WHAT PEOPLE ARE SAYING ABOUT

SKILLS FOR LIFE

"Mike Jarvis and Jonathan Peck have assembled the most versatile, mobile and user-friendly career and life-counseling guidebook that I have ever read."

— Ralph C. Martin, II, Partner, Bingham McCutchen

"*Skills for Life* captures the essence of success in a book that is manageable in its size, insightful in its content, and illuminating in its use of personal experiences."

— Matthew Allain, Principal, The AYCO Company, LP

"The book soars without ever losing touch with the ground. Also, it is eloquent but easy to read. Its chapters are truly a road map to personal and business success."

— Robert J. McGuire, Counsel, Morvillo Abramovitz,
Former Commissioner, NYPD

"*Skills for Life* is a wonderful handbook for success. Great story lessons from a great coach."

— Donna Shalala, President, University of Miami

"Coach Jarvis and Jonathan Peck provide practical solutions to the many challenges we all face in our daily lives in *Skills for Life* — a must-read for anyone who desires to succeed in life."

— Gregory W. Meeks, Member of Congress,
Sixth District, New York

"The life skills brilliantly presented in this book should be hard wired into every person by the age of 16. Had I been so fortunate, many mistakes would have been avoided. Unquestionably, my life's journey would have been provided a powerful jump start."

— Peter Cove, Founder/President, America Works

"After reading *Skills for Life,* I feel this a must-read for any coach at any level."
— **Morgan Wootten, Head Basketball Coach,**
De Matha Catholic High School

"Coach Jarvis and Jonathan Peck teach life's Code of Conduct with good judgment and common sense. Their book contains everything your mother tried to teach you."
— **John Horn, V.P., Pinkerton Consulting and Investigations**

"*Skills for Life* offers essential practical advice that should be heeded by anyone who wishes to live a life of consequence."
— **Craig Evan Klafter, President, St. Catherine's College**
(Oxford) Foundation

"*Skills for Life* scores big as a fundamental primer for audiences of all ages, backgrounds and needs. I am impressed! The book is correctly labeled a "coaching manual for life" and really hits a bull's-eye with the 'Ten Fundamentals for Success'."
— **Sally Cunningham, Executive Director, National Council of**
Youth Sports

"With our lives in constant transition and renewal, the *Skills for Life* instructional guide is for all of us. Great read."
— **John Stoeckle, M.D., Harvard Medical School,**
Massachusetts General Hospital

"This book teaches the young how to play the game of life, and for those of us who are older, makes us reflect upon how to be a better person."
— **Robert H. Prince, Jr., Former G.M., Massachusetts**
Bay Transportation Authority

"If it takes a village to raise a child, then *Skills for Life* represents the best of the village's wisdom regarding what it takes to be successful in life, personally as well as professionally."
— **Grady B. Hedgespeth, President/Executive Director,**
The ICA Group

"I was introduced to the Skills for Life progam as a college student athlete; its lessons are the foundation of my professional and personal life."

— David F. Wallace, V.P./Sales, Chevy Chase Bank

"Skills and competencies are a challenge to teach. Wisdom is far harder. Through the sharing of personal experience, *Skills for Life* teaches and shares both the skills and the wisdom needed not only by athletes but by us all."

— Fr. Donald Harrington, President, St. John's University

"You won't find this kind of information in any other book today! *Skills for Life* is fresh, new and REAL — a must-read for those who don't know where they are going and those that have been there."

— Mikel Oglesby, Former Assistant G.M., Massachusetts Bay Transportation Authority

"*Skills for Life* captures components of the lifetime equation in a manner to which fresh young minds and geezers like me can mutually relate."

— L. A. Wansley, Managing Director/Corporate Security, American Airlines

"*Skills for Life* provides an outstanding 'game plan' for young people to approach the world in which they live. It is a must for all of us who work with and care about today's youth."

— Ian McCaw, Director of Athletics, UMass-Amherst

"*Skills for Life* should be made a mandatory part of every high school senior's curriculum. It is an invaluable reference tool that should be consulted as the gospel!"

— Robert Ades, Robert A. Ades & Associates, P.C.

"The real story in becoming successful in life profiles skills like . . . character, attitude, spirituality, and basic communication. An insightful book — a must-read for all young adults today."

— Dennis Jackson, Founder/President, P.L.A.Y., Inc.

"One should not make the mistake of assuming this book is about basketball. Students, athletes, job seekers and CEOs alike will benefit from its tips on how to succeed in any of life's endeavors."

— Rick Taylor, Director of Athletics,
Northwestern University

"Anyone in the 'people business' needs this book."

— Mike McKay, Senior Policy Advisor to
U.S. Representative Gregory Meeks

"It is an excellent piece, filled with many practical items of advice and elements of wisdom which, I believe, not only make good sense, but which I have strived to adopt."

— Wayne A. Budd, Executive V.P./General Counsel,
John Hancock Financial Services

"*Skills for Life* is filled with practical wisdom. There are gold nuggets between the front and back covers just waiting to be mined."

— Tom Fitzpatrick, Former Communications Executive

"*Skills for Life* stresses the essentials — character, respect, discipline, and attitude. It is absolutely essential for those in high school, college, or just starting out in their career. The book offers young people a way to true success."

— C. Maury Devine, Former Mobil Corporation Executive

"The book takes an uncomplicated approach to dealing with ourselves and our relationships with others."

— George M. Murphy, Virtual Security, Inc.

"*Skills for Life* is a great primer for people of all ages and experience. The underlying message of taking responsibility for one's personal development is one that applies to people both young and old."

— Carolyn Schlie Femovich, Executive Director,
Patriot League

"*Skills for Life* provides an invaluable road map for winning in the 'real' world. Not only is it a great read for young folks starting out, it is a reminder for those of us who've been around for a while."

— Bill Cunningham, President, Hallcrest Systems Inc.

"*Skills for Life* is full of insights and practical suggestions on how to grow and develop as a person. I was struck by how beneficial this book would be for my son."

— Jim Haney, Executive Director, National Association
of Basketball Coaches

"*Skills for Life* is a results-producing plan that covers the critical elements on your pathway to success and prosperity."

— Jack Carew, Best-selling Author,
You'll Never Get No For An Answer

"Mike Jarvis and Jonathan Peck have distilled the keys to success into easy-to-apply principles. *Skills for Life* represents a bank of knowledge from which people from all walks of life can surely benefit."

— Bill Wennington, Coordinator/Player Relation Program,
Chicago Bulls

"You have been able to capture in one book all of the foundational principles needed to frame success in personal and social interactions, principles of life that originally came from home and church."

— Annie Mair, Principal, Cleveland Elementary School,
Washington, D.C.

"*Skills for Life* is reader-friendly and provides great examples, stories, and worksheets to guide the novice or more mature person on how to succeed in life. The advice is first-rate, providing clear insights and practical guidance. . . . strategies that anyone can use."

— Barbara Fritze, V.P. for Enrollment and Educational
Services, Gettysburg College

"I found it a very impressive book. It can be read by an individual seeking personal guidance on life situations or used as a 'text' for a course in which adults can provide young people an opportunity to discuss such issues."
— Gary Strickler, Director of Athletics, Boston University

"*Skills for Life* is both spiritual and practical. That rare combination should speak to and help a broad spectrum of people at all stages of development."
— Janell Phillips, V.P., Brown Brothers Harriman

"The best thing about *Skills for Life* is that it's an easy read and every page has a thought to ponder and remember. The layout is unique and comfortable as well."
— Larry Michael, V.P., Executive Producer/Sports,
Westwood One

"Jarvis and Peck have given us a game plan to succeed in life. Their easy-to-read text will help young people to develop good character and acquire a sense of self that will make them the best person they can possibly be."
— Richard Lapchick, Chair, DeVos Sport Business
Management Program,
University of Central Florida

"*Skills for Life* provides excellent advice for self-assessment, personal development, and knowledge building. The combination of business theory with sports examples and life experiences provides an effective blend. *Skills for Life* covers areas broadly, yet provides enough specific detail to appeal to a wide audience."
— John Glover, former V.P./Security, Bristol-Myers Squibb

"As Coach Jarvis and Jon Peck make clear in the book, wins and losses are not the final measure of a person. It is character that defines who you are, and *Skills for Life* lays out a simple game plan for the development of character. I can't imagine a more valuable gift."
— Jonathan Hock, Hock Films

SKILLS FOR LIFE

SKILLS FOR LIFE

THE FUNDAMENTALS
YOU NEED TO SUCCEED

MIKE JARVIS

AND

JONATHAN PECK

SKILLS FOR LIFE LLC
BOSTON • NEW YORK

ISBN 0-9724311-1-X (cl.)
ISBN 0-9724311-0-1 (pb.)

Published in the United States by Skills for Life LLC
Distributed by Client Distribution Services

Visit our Web site at www.skillsforlife.com

10 9 8 7 6 5 4 3 2 1

PRINTED IN THE UNITED STATES OF AMERICA

To our mothers — both named Dorothy —
who gave us our foundation.
And to the many people we've met on our journey
who have contributed to our
better understanding of the
Skills for Life.

CONTENTS

How You Look

How You Perform

WHERE DO YOU GO
FROM HERE?

FOREWORD

Skills for Life offers practical advice to help the reader succeed — in business, in relationships, in life. It is a how-to book for those committed to helping others realize their full potential, or a reference guide for individuals who still consider themselves a "work in progress." Its authors, Mike Jarvis and Jonathan Peck, have learned the lessons offered through lifelong involvement with the worlds of sports and business.

Mike Jarvis, successful men's basketball coach at St. John's University in New York, is a highly respected national sports figure. Jonathan Peck is a management and communications consultant with over thirty-five years of experience building and expanding businesses, teaching, and developing the Skills for Life program.

In 1985, when Jarvis assumed his first collegiate head basketball coaching position at Boston University, he quickly realized that his players were capable of both handling their academic programs and responding to his basketball demands. However, he observed that they all had a narrow focus regarding the future and were, by and large, clueless as to what it takes to be successful in life. He shared his concerns with his friend Jonathan Peck, and together they created Skills for Life, a program to teach student-athletes about life after sports, and to expose them to established business people who demonstrate first hand the validity of its concepts.

Skills for Life is the natural evolution of the "Shoot

Straight" program Jarvis and Joe Colannino created for the youth of Cambridge, Massachusetts, in the 1970s. He used the game of basketball as a vehicle to teach young people about the important issues of life. Throughout his coaching career, Jarvis has returned again and again to the key concepts of the Skills for Life program to foster his players' growth and development — not only in the basketball arena — but in the arena of life.

The Skills for Life philosophy has served his players well. During Jarvis's tenure at Cambridge Rindge & Latin High School, all but two of his players moved on to college. The remaining two became a policeman and a firefighter. The graduation rate for his college players is similarly high.

Jarvis's conviction that *Skills for Life* should be available to more than just a select group of student-athletes was a driving force in the program's expansion. Peck took Skills for Life on the road and, for some seventeen years, has conveyed its concepts to thousands of high school and college students. The program has also been used to assist organizations with employee development, and by individuals seeking advice at all stages of their careers.

Jarvis moved from his head coaching position at Boston University to George Washington University in Washington, D.C., to his current assignment at St. John's University in New York. Yet he and Peck continued to refine the Skills for Life concepts as audience needs and the changing times required.

Skills for Life reflects its creators' belief that part of the fabric which holds our society together is the instinct to lend a helping hand. They came to this conviction on parallel routes — Jarvis in education and coaching and Peck in business and teaching — and from similar backgrounds. Both were raised by a single parent in a home in which money was far from plentiful. They learned the value of a solid work ethic at a young age. They were both blessed with strong mothers, caring teachers, and wise mentors to guide them along their way. The two committed themselves early in their adult lives to providing similar support to whomever they could.

Now the authors are "giving back" by imparting the practical wisdom of their collective experience — the fundamentals of the "game of life" — to a broader audience. Anyone who has attempted to shepherd another human being through a process of growth and development knows well the difficulty of the task, and how helpful it is to have an ally. The *Skills for Life* book is that ally.

Each chapter deals with fundamental skill sets that must be mastered in order to succeed and excel in today's complex society. The chapters open with a statement of purpose and proceed with a discussion of the concepts to be mastered, as well as practical applications of the skill. Mike Jarvis enlivens each chapter with anecdotes about real-life situations — his own and others — that illustrate the subject skill. A summary page closes the chapter with easy-to-follow suggestions and thought provoking questions.

Winning or losing a "game" is not the central thesis. The way you go about trying to achieve; the way you treat yourself and others; the manner in which you handle stress, difficult situations, and change; how you execute your plan; and the measure of peace you can achieve — these are the concepts of Skills for Life. Jarvis and Peck tell a story replete with successes, failures, compassion and humor that will resonate with every reader and affirm the following:

THE QUALITY OF A PERSON'S LIFE IS IN DIRECT PRO-
PORTION TO THEIR COMMITMENT TO EXCELLENCE
REGARDLESS OF THEIR CHOSEN FELD OF ENDEAVOR.
— VINCE LOMBARDI, LEGENDARY COACH,
GREEN BAY PACKERS FOOTBALL TEAM

ACKNOWLEDGMENTS

Skills for Life in book form is the result of 17 years of on-the-job training perfecting our presentation, and three years of writing, editing, and perfecting our manuscript. Many people have been of enormous help along the way — we hope our list is all-inclusive. Any omissions should be attributed to lapse of memory rather than lack of gratitude.

Thanks must be extended to the thousands of Skills for Life students, student-athletes, teachers, and coaches that we have worked with throughout the country. Their engagement with the program enabled us to improve our content and delivery, and provided us with ongoing reality checks. Of course, all of the young men and women who played for Coach Jarvis over the years, and demonstrated many of the skills included herein, are among those who deserve recognition.

We would like to acknowledge the efforts of our friend, Grady Hedgespeth, who helped the Skills for Life "movement" get started. He instructed hundreds of students in its basic tenets, and continues to enliven our presentations with his unique insights and experience. We must also recognize the efforts of two others who have injected a fresh perspective — Mike Oglesby and David Wallace.

Over the years, the Skills for Life Program has benefited from the wisdom and business acumen of independent advisors: Jack Cowan, Bob Cumings, Bob Glover, Bob Jones, Dave McNitt, Chuck Merin, Jim Nentwig, Dennis O'Connor, Walter Palmer, Charles Rogovin, Tom Rosenbloom, and Joe Rosetti. Their suggestions are always insightful and on point.

We would be remiss if we did not mention those colleges that afforded us opportunities to perfect our presentation, including: Boston College, Clark University, College of the Holy Cross, Fordham University, Seton Hall University,

Springfield College, UMass-Boston, Boston University, George Washington University, and St. John's University.

Among the collegiate coaches who saw the value of the Skills for Life® concept early on and shared it with their student-athletes are: Ed Bilik, George Blaney, P. J. Carlesimo, Nick Macarchuk, Lawrence Mangino, Billy Raynor, and Dennis Wolff. Special thanks are extended to Jim O'Brien and Charlie Titus whose extra efforts helped immeasurably.

Two others — Boston Police Commissioner Paul Evans and Dennis Jackson, Director of P.L.A.Y., Inc. of Holyoke, Massachusetts — saw the value of Skills for Life and use it as a tool to expand the horizons of the at-risk and college-or-workplace-bound youth they serve. We are privileged to broaden our audience to include these young people.

Our book journey began by seeking some sage advice from knowledgeable business and literary folk. We received, and continue to receive, just such advice from: Peter Cove, C. Maury Devine, Jack Greene, David LaCamera, and Betsy Lerner. A special thanks to Robert Levine, whose guiding hand got us underway, and David Peck, who helped with the initial draft and organization.

We subjected some friends and acquaintances to early draft chapters; thanks to those who took the time to read and offer valuable critiques. They include: Ron Brown, Wally Bruckner, Bill Cunningham, Bishop William Deveaux, David Dottin, Gene DiFilippo, Karen Ercole, Tom Fitzpatrick, Robert German, Mark Hall, Steve Harper, Scott Harshbarger, John Horn, Don Lane, Walter Leonard, Don Lupfer, Bill Maloney, Frank McGovern, Mike McKay, Keith Motley, Richard Mullins, Tony Pierce, Steve Scheer, Gary Strickler, Steve Vantine, Lesley Visser, Larry Wansley, and Stu Wheeler.

We are indebted to other reviewers who significantly improved the material through careful edits, suggestions for different topic approaches, or corrections to text that missed its mark. Our thanks to: Matthew Allain, Mark Armiento, Gail Errera, Reverend Floyd Flake, Joe Geller, Father James Maher, Ralph C. Martin II, Hank Shafran, and Gillian Gattie, who spent hours poring over many of the chapters; Chris White for his encouragement and vision; and Ursula Mika for all her hard work and support.

When we decided to tackle the publishing of *Skills for Life* ourselves, we turned to Susan Hayes. She kept us focused on the process; our book was much improved after her input. Cover designer Steve Snider and photographer Bill Miles made us look better than we are.

Thanks to everyone who played a part in making *Skills for Life* a reality.

A very special thank you to our friend,
Kathy Synnott, whose dedication, commitment,
and incredible skills made a signifiant contribution
to the development of this book.

GETTING STARTED

TO OUR READERS

"LIFE IS A DECATHLON — YOU MUST BE GOOD
AT MORE THAN ONE EVENT."

— MICHAEL J. McGOVERN, ESQ.

Whoever picks up a copy of *Skills for Life* may justifiably ask what prompted its authors to create yet another how-to book. The answer is quite simple. *Skills for Life* is the heartfelt response to the one question we have been asked repeatedly over seventeen years of presenting the Skills for Life program and more than thirty-five years of coaching, consulting, teaching, and working with people trying to succeed.

When we present Skills for Life programs in high school, college, or corporate settings, we find that at every stop along the way, the issue foremost in the minds of our attendees is the same. The words used to express their anxiety may vary but, in essence, each audience asks, "What does it take to succeed in the 'real' world?"

The fact that our audiences articulate this concern over and over makes it clear that many are not being armed with the tools they need to face the "real world" with confidence and enthusiasm. Our audiences want basic instruction on how to make their way in the world — how to look, act, sound, and be. They need to learn more about the skills critical to success in school, in work, in life.

Thus, *Skills for Life* is written for anyone who has tried to teach — e.g., parents, coaches, teachers, mentors, and employers — or anyone who has tried to learn, e.g., students, young people starting a career, and those stalled personally and/or professionally. Both audiences will benefit from the advice contained within *Skills for Life*. The book is a coaching manual for life.

Is our formula foolproof? No. Does it provide all the answers? No. But it can help in two ways. First, the book enables "coaches" to identify areas of concern, give advice with a greater degree of confidence, and launch the all-important communication process. Second, "players" can apply the lessons directly to their own lives.

We have tried to offer clear, direct information concerning the skills that we consider "the fundamentals." We're not claiming to be experts at any one of the topics covered. We're just two people who wish to share practical insight and know-how that has served us well and enabled us to enjoy a measure of success and happiness. It is our hope that every reader of this book will extract some useful information from it that they can put into action. At the very least, we hope the reader will remember the following secret of success:

SUCCESS

Success is not reserved for the talented. It is not in the high I.Q. Not in the gifted birth. Not in the best equipment. Not even in ability. Success is almost totally dependent upon drive, focus and persistence. The energy required to make an extra effort, or try another approach, is the secret.

BEFORE YOU BEGIN

On the next few pages you will find a Skills for Life Personal Inventory. Each set of questions in the inventory (adapted from material developed by Connie Jarvis) corresponds to a chapter of the book. We think this is a useful exercise for everyone — young or old, seasoned or not. Your honest answer to each question will give you a good idea of the areas in which you, or the person you are helping, could stand some improvement.

A careful analysis of the inventory results will identify those areas in which the greatest work is necessary. The corresponding chapters of *Skills for Life,* then, are the ones that should be read and digested first. Then readers can move on to chapters covering skills for which they have some demonstrated aptitude, but that need improvement.

We hope that the Personal Inventory will encourage readers to develop an individual approach to *Skills for Life.* There is no one prescribed way to make the most of the information this book provides. It has been specifically organized to be used either as a reference for skill areas, or as a comprehensive curriculum for self-improvement.

Skills for Life has been a singular passion of ours for a number of years. We have enjoyed using it as a vehicle for forming connections with thousands of people anxious to learn more about making the most of their lives. We hope that our passion comes through in the book and that our readers enjoy using it as a road map for their own life journeys. Good luck and have fun!

SKILLS FOR LIFE
PERSONAL INVENTORY

CHARACTER

	0	1	2	3	4
1. I take responsibility for my actions.					✓
2. I honor my commitments.				✓	
3. I demonstrate concern for others					✓
4. When in doubt about what to do, I try to do the right thing.					✓

Total __

ATTITUDE

	0	1	2	3	4
1. Whatever I do, I do it with enthusiasm.			✓		
2. I try not to let setbacks stand in my way.			✓		
3. I try not to take things too seriously.		✓			
4. I take something positive from every experience I have.			✓		

Total __

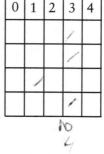

GETTING ALONG

1. I regularly try to make people feel good.
2. I offer helpful criticism, not sarcasm.
3. I give praise and thanks to others.
4. I respect the ideas of others, regardless
   of who they are.

0	1	2	3	4
			✓	
			✓	
			✓	
			✓	

12

Total __

SPIRITUALITY

1. I feed my soul with helping others.
2. I believe a greater power can guide me.
3. I count my blessings regularly.
4. I take time every day to think about the
   purpose of my life.

0	1	2	3	4
	✓			
		✓		
		✓		
				✓

Total __   11

APPEARANCE

1. I keep my clothing and shoes neat.
2. I try to be well-groomed at all times.
3. I am committed to daily exercise.
4. I try to eat well, avoid junk food.

0	1	2	3	4
		✓		
			✓	
✓				
		✓		

Total __ 9

COSTUME

	0	1	2	3	4
1. I try to have my clothes fit the occasion.			✓		
2. I choose clothes in appropriate styles.				✓	
3. I choose basic styles that will last.				✓	
4. When dressing for work, I stay away from loud ties, sheer blouses, flashy socks or stockings, etc.					✓

Total __

BASIC COMMUNICATION

	0	1	2	3	4
1. I know how to to pay attention.				✓	
2. I speak slowly and clearly. I speak well.				✓	
3. I keep my language appropriate.					✓
4. I try to make a good first impression.					✓

Total __ 14

WORK WITH A PLAN

	0	1	2	3	4
1. I set specific and realistic goals.				✓	
2. I make lists regularly.			✓		
3. I stick to my task schedules.			✓		
4. I try always to have a back-up plan.			✓		

Total __ 12

MATTERS OF MONEY

	0	1	2	3	4
1. I set up a budget and try to stick to it.	/				
2. I pay my bills on time.	/				
3. I use credit cards with caution.	/				
4. I keep careful track of my finances, balance my checkbook.	/				

Total __ 4

GIVING BACK

	0	1	2	3	4
1. I am sensitive to the needs of others				/	
2. I make a difference whenever I can.				/	
3. I know where to go to help people.			/		
4. I contribute my time or money whenever possible.			/		

Total __ 7 6

REMEMBER: IT'S NOT ABOUT THE SCORE,
SCORES ARE FOR GAMES.
IT'S ABOUT MAKING YOURSELF
THE BEST PERSON YOU CAN BE.

WHO YOU ARE

CHARACTER

"You can easily judge the character of a person by how he treats those who can do nothing for him or to him."

— Malcolm Forbes,
Business Leader & founder of Forbes magazine

Society's foundation — how we deal with important issues, how we treat people, our laws, the values we hold dear, etc. — is in great part built on character — individual or collective. Character contributes more to what we do, and the person we become, than wealth, intelligence, religion, race, or ethnicity. Our everyday actions speak volumes about character. Are we responsible? Do we look for the easy way out? Are we truthful and forthright? Do we manage to cope with adversity? As we mature, we quickly realize that the stronger our character, the better our life can be. In this chapter, we explore character — its importance, its qualities, its impact on our everyday existence, and how we can attempt to improve it. Character is the heart of our existence.

WHAT IS CHARACTER?

The *Oxford American Dictionary* defines character as "the collective qualities or characteristics, especially mental and moral, that distinguish a person." Character, in short, defines who you are.

Character is not something you can feel, smell, hear, or see. Yet, having good character represents the single most important ingredient for shaping a meaningful and successful life.

Character is not personality, although your personality may give clues about your character. It's who you are . . . even when you're asleep. It is that collection of values, beliefs, and actions that outlines your personal profile. It is what you grow into as you grow up, and it is what others evaluate you by: "He's a stand-up kind of guy." "She's extremely loyal." "They'll come through in the tough times."

Character plays more of a role in your personal and business life than any other aspect of your being. Children are in the process of developing character, which is why they change their beliefs and their behavior from day to day. Adults are supposed to have formed their character, although we continue to refine it throughout life.

⭐

Mike: While coaching at George Washington University, I was fortunate to develop a relationship with Arnold "Red" Auerbach, architect of professional basketball's great dynasty—the Boston Celtics—and a GWU alumnus. I vividly recall his saying that one of the key elements in the Celtics' formula for success was to "recruit character, not characters."

I try to follow his advice and look for players who want to work hard, and look forward to being challenged—educationally, culturally, and socially, as well as physically. While others may have valued them solely on the basis of their basketball skills, their worth to my team is based upon their values.

Sometimes, however, recruitment has nothing to do with the addition of character to the roster. Take Andre Stanley for example, a "walk-on" with the 2001–2002 St. John's squad who received no athletic scholarship.

Andre's story is remarkable because of the obstacles he overcomes on a daily basis just to get to practice. He lives in Brooklyn and commutes to the university which is in Jamaica, New York. This is no ordinary commute. He gets up at 5:00 A.M., walks several blocks to the train, rides the subway for an hour, then switches to a bus to ride from Kew Gardens to our campus. He is usually first to arrive at our 7:30 A.M. practice.

Basketball has been Andre's passion since he was a youngster. While in junior college, his skills drew the attention of East Carolina University, and they offered him a full athletic scholarship. However, before he was off to college, Andre had to take his mother, a severe diabetic, to the hospital emergency room, where he was told that her condition necessitated amputation of a leg. What would his mother do? How would she get around? Who would care for her? And, what would Andre do about his dream of playing college basketball? He knew his mother needed him and would miss him terribly, so in a decision he termed a "no-brainer," he opted to stay at home and become a day student at St. John's.

Andre didn't waste time complaining about his lost scholarship. He just set his sights on becoming a member of the St. John's team. In so doing, he became our hardest worker and most diligent student of the game. He was a pleasure to have on our team. Over the season, his fellow players learned more about character and personal responsibility from his example than I could ever hope to teach them.

Andre's hard work did not go unrewarded. He was the first walk-on player in twenty-three years at St. John's to make the starting line-up and contribute to the team's success.

There is an important postscript to Andre's story. He was one of the focal points of ESPN's documentary about the Red Storm's 2001—2002 campaign entitled *The Season: St. John's Basketball.* A Wall Street financial professional, Mitch Katz, viewed the program and was moved by Andre's story and impressed by his commitment — so impressed that he offered him a summer internship. Andre accepted the offer and may be on his way to a permanent position upon graduation. Clearly, Mitch Katz agrees with Red Auerbach that one should recruit character not characters.

QUALITIES OF CHARACTER

Character involves many qualities we may not be able to see and, in many cases, do not employ as often as we should, virtues such as those listed by William J. Bennett, in his best seller *The Book of Virtues* (1993):

Compassion	Loyalty	Courage
Perseverance	Faith	Responsibility
Friendship	Honesty	Self-Discipline
	Work	

We identify character by observing how people apply these qualities in their treatment of others and themselves. Character may be invisible — but we see it in action every day. Abraham Lincoln once said, "Character is like a tree and reputation like its shadow. The shadow is what we think of it; the tree is the real thing." Do you have any or all of these character traits? Do you know what these qualities are? It is easy enough to find out. Take some time and let the following questions sink in — reflect on your answers.

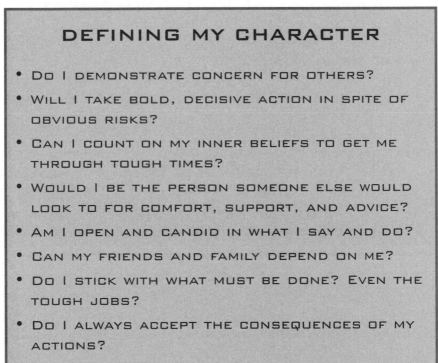

DEFINING MY CHARACTER

- DO I DEMONSTRATE CONCERN FOR OTHERS?

- WILL I TAKE BOLD, DECISIVE ACTION IN SPITE OF OBVIOUS RISKS?

- CAN I COUNT ON MY INNER BELIEFS TO GET ME THROUGH TOUGH TIMES?

- WOULD I BE THE PERSON SOMEONE ELSE WOULD LOOK TO FOR COMFORT, SUPPORT, AND ADVICE?

- AM I OPEN AND CANDID IN WHAT I SAY AND DO?

- CAN MY FRIENDS AND FAMILY DEPEND ON ME?

- DO I STICK WITH WHAT MUST BE DONE? EVEN THE TOUGH JOBS?

- DO I ALWAYS ACCEPT THE CONSEQUENCES OF MY ACTIONS?

- AM I ALWAYS UNDER CONTROL?

- DO I PUT IN EXTRA EFFORT TO GET THINGS DONE?

Mike: One of the strongest lessons I learned early on in life was to be dependable and finish what I start. I learned this lesson through observing just the opposite behavior in my father, Richard Jarvis.

My dad was not a daily presence in our lives, yet he lived nearby. He was a skilled carpenter, and demand for his workmanship was great. However, he had a drinking problem. He left a trail of unfinished carpentry jobs, as the money customers paid him often went for alcohol instead of building materials.

He was also irresponsible in promises he made to his children. I cannot count the times I waited hours for him to take me on a promised fishing trip, only to have him never show. I vowed I would try never to walk away from a commitment when I grew up, and I have tried to stick to it through my adult life.

There have been occasions when I have been approached to accept new positions, with greater challenges and financial rewards. On some occasions, when the time was appropriate for my family, and the goals set for my current team had been achieved, I made the change.

At other times, the change would have been disruptive not only to me, but, more importantly, to those for whom I bore a major responsibility. I could not expect a university, or its players, to make a commitment to me if I would not do the same for them. I just could not leave until I felt the job was done.

CHARACTER IN ACTION

To some extent, every one of our actions reveals our character. If we are always blaming someone else for our mistakes, we demonstrate an unwillingness to accept responsibility. If we owe people money, but continually avoid them, we show how little weight our word carries. If we are only fair-weather friends, our loyalty becomes a matter of question. The examples are endless—we're sure you can think of many others.

If you wonder what an intended action might say about your character, apply what we call the "mother test." That is, ask yourself, "What would my mother say?" before you follow any course of action.

Character, in short, is revealed in everything we do, and in everything we see or read about other people.

Mike: As a young man, I recall reading about Rosa Parks and wondering if I would ever have enough character to stand up for my beliefs as courageously as she did.

On December 1, 1955, Mrs. Parks boarded a bus in Montgomery, Alabama, after a hard day's work and sat in the first row of the "colored section." A white man boarded the bus and ordered her to give up her seat to him. Rosa refused, not because she was so tired from work, but because she was tired of the treatment she endured every day. The time had come to stand firm against the indignities and injustices of racism and segregation.

Mrs. Parks was arrested, tried, and convicted of violating Montgomery's segregation laws. However,

*her simple act of courage inspired a bus boycott in
the city and led to the formation of a civil rights
organization, the Montgomery Improvement
Association, that chose Martin Luther King, Jr., a
young minister, as its president. Her strength of
character inspired others to join the fight against segregation and racism. From the first time I heard the
Rosa Parks story, she has remained for me a shining
example of character in action.*

DISCOVERING YOUR OWN CHARACTER

So what does any of this have to do with you? Everything!

Like every other person, you must know yourself: who you
are and what your character is. And, you must understand that
your character charts your direction and determines what
becomes of you for the rest of your life.

Character is reflected in everything that speaks about
you, from how you relate to others, to relationships you have
with family and friends, to contributions you make in your
community.

Character is reflected in what others say about you when
asked to give a reference for school or business. For example,
"He's a solid worker," or "She really produces. She has a good
work ethic." Or, "He's not terribly reliable. I don't trust him
with a lot of responsibility."

Can you change your character? Yes — but the older you
get, the harder it is to change.

How do you find that character? The easiest way to determine your own character is to look at your relationships—with
family, teammates, girl and boy friends, other adults. What
distinguishes those relationships? Love, trust, friendship? Or,

distrust, selfishness, impatience. You be the judge.

⭐

Mike: My relationship with my family had a significant impact on the development of my character. I was one of four children—the "middle kid"—with an older brother and sister, Richard and Trudy, and a younger brother, Stephen. Ours was a single-parent household, and my mother, Dorothy Jarvis, had to work two to three jobs at a time to keep the family going. She worked in a factory, cleaned houses — whatever it took to put clothes on our backs and food on the table.

My older brother—the real athlete in the family— never had a chance to realize his full athletic potential because he had to assume the paternal role for his younger siblings. My older sister, a person of grace, beauty, and intelligence, had to become our "associate mother," taking on adult responsibilities at far too young an age.

As a short kid with serious weight issues, it was hard for me to figure out what my place was in the family structure. So, whether consciously or not, I set out to achieve the athletic and academic goals that my older brother and sister never had the opportunity to achieve. Given the fact that I had neither his athletic gifts, nor her God-given intelligence, the drive to succeed was fueled by the example of perseverance my mother provided.

Without the influence of my family as I was growing up, I doubt whether the qualities of character they displayed daily—love, generosity, self-respect, responsibility, and self-discipline — would have been woven so tightly into the fabric of my life.

CHARACTER MEETS CHALLENGE

The real test of character is when you're challenged, when life is not going as you think it should, when you are, as they say, "up against it." Basically, there are two types of challenges that come to us in life:

1. The challenge of being prepared, understanding our role in life, our work, the importance of educating ourselves, and planning for the life we think we want to live. To some degree, we have control over this type of challenge.

2. The challenge of dealing with events that occur and over which we may have absolutely no control— the death of a loved one or family member, having a serious illness, loss of a job, or being involved in a natural catastrophe. Often, we are powerless to avoid these personal misfortunes.

Having a plan to point yourself in the right direction is a big help with the first type of challenge. (See *Work with a Plan.*) Dealing with the second type of challenge, however, is where your character comes into play and your measure as a person can be taken.

OVERCOMING ADVERSITY

One of the toughest challenges in life is facing and overcoming adversity, regardless of how large or small the problem. Setbacks in all aspects of life are commonplace, and you aren't really a fully developed person until you've worked your way through difficult times. It's your response to these situations that really counts. Your attitude (See *Attitude,* page 29.) will help your approach to hardship, but your character is what will enable you to prevail.

We've all been in bad situations — unemployment, a dead-end job, a difficult relationship, or chronic illness. This is life; these are the circumstances many people have to deal with on a daily basis. Our character plays a pivotal role in how we respond to the troubles and helps to determine whether or not the outcomes can or will be favorable.

Let's say you're in a bad situation at work or in your personal life. You can do one of two things. You can criticize those you believe to be responsible, excluding yourself, of course. Or, you can simply do the very best you can under the circumstances by understanding the true problem and eliminating negative thoughts.

If you continue to do the best you can through the strength of your character, whether the situation turns around or not is secondary. When character and challenge converge, your actions in trying circumstances are a clear indicator of the quality of your character.

There are a number of important things to remember when creating an action plan for dealing with difficulties or trying times:

ACTION PLAN FOR "HARD TIMES"

- MAINTAIN A POSITIVE ATTITUDE.

- DON'T TAKE "THE EASY WAY OUT. MAKE THE DIFFICULT DECISIONS WHEN NECESSARY.

- ACCEPT DEFEAT FOR WHAT IT IS. SOME DEFEATS OR LOSSES ARE INESCAPABLE; LEARN FROM THEM. IF MISTAKES HAVE BEEN MADE, FIND OUT WHY AND MOVE FORWARD WITH A DETERMINATION NOT TO REPEAT THEM.

- ASK FOR HELP. SHARING YOUR PROBLEMS WITH SOMEONE MAKES THEM SEEM LESS OF A BURDEN. A FRESH OUTLOOK ALWAYS HELPS.

- HAVE FAITH. HAVING FAITH IN A POWER GREATER THAN YOURSELF CAN HELP YOU SURVIVE, AND PERHAPS BENEFIT FROM, THE MOST DIFFICULT CHALLENGES.

Mike: I read about a young athlete by the name of Scott Carlson in the Boston Globe *who weathered adversity in a particularly admirable way. His story conveys the notion of character far more powerfully than anything we could write in this book.*

Scott Carlson has been a triathlete, surfer, expert skier, guitar player, and software expert. He was a former training partner of Karen Smyers, a world-class triathlete. Just when he was at the top of his game in every aspect of his life, he was diagnosed with ALS (amyotrophic lateral sclerosis), more commonly known as "Lou Gehrig's disease."

The disease attacks the nerve cells of the brain and spinal cord, gradually incapacitating its victims. ALS forced Carlson to give up all his athletic pursuits, his job, and driving a car. He could neither eat nor shower by himself. No cure exists and the disease is ultimately fatal.

Rather than mourn his past life, Carlson chose to live his present one as fully as possible. He created a presentation for young people called "Adversity Leads to Success" (using the initials of his disease). He advises them to to be more grateful for the life they lead and appreciate what they have rather than long for what they don't have.

I can think of no better example of how character can enable a person to prevail in the face of the harshest reality imaginable.

CHARACTER SUMMARY

Character is the core of who you are—your cornerstone. Can it be improved? Yes — with awareness, attention and hard work. Your character will determine your destiny. We often paraphrase Charles Reade, nineteenth-century British novelist, when we present "character watchwords" at our Skills for Life programs.

- *Watch your thoughts; they become words.*
- *Watch your words; they become actions.*
- *Watch your actions; they become habits.*
- *Watch your habits; they become character.*
- *Watch your character; it becomes destiny.*

CHARACTER REMINDERS

- Character is developed by you but defined by others.
- Let a strong character determine your reputation.
- Examine your own character regularly. Ask yourself the series of questions mentioned on page 17 (Defining My Character).
- When in doubt as to the right thing to do, apply the "mother test."
- Ask a friend to give you an honest evaluation of your character, and which areas might be improved.
- When applicable, follow the "Action Plan for Hard Times."

CHARACTER QUESTIONS

1. How would others who know me well describe
    my character?

    _____

    _____

    _____

    _____

    _____

2. What can I do to begin taking more responsibility for
    my actions?

    _____

    _____

    _____

    _____

    _____

3. What is my approach to difficult situations and how
    can it be improved?

    _____

    _____

    _____

    _____

    _____

ATTITUDE

"I'M CONVINCED THAT LIFE IS 10% WHAT HAPPENS TO ME AND 90% HOW I REACT TO IT. AND SO IT IS WITH YOU — WE ARE IN CHARGE OF OUR ATTITUDES."

— CHARLES SWINDOLL,
AUTHOR OF **STRENGTHENING YOUR GRIP**

A POSITIVE ATTITUDE IS THE MOST IMPORTANT PIECE OF MENTAL EQUIPMENT WE DRAW UPON EVERY DAY. WHEN WE ARE CHILDREN, WE ARE ENTHUSIASTIC ABOUT EVERYTHING — NEW EXPERIENCES ARE A CAUSE OF DELIGHT, NOT ALARM. AS ADULTS, WE OFTEN HAVE A TENDENCY TO CONSIDER ONLY THE DOWNSIDE OF PRESENT OR FUTURE CIRCUMSTANCES, PROVING THE PENNSYLVANIA DUTCH SAYING THAT "WE GET TOO SOON OLD AND TOO LATE SMART." WE SOMETIMES ALLOW NEGATIVE FEELINGS OR LACK OF SELF-ESTEEM TO CLOUD OUR OUTLOOK. SO, WHAT TO DO? WE MUST CONCENTRATE ON ACQUIRING A POSITIVE ATTITUDE; IT IS AN EFFORT THAT NEEDS CONSTANT ATTENTION.

THE POSITIVE ATTITUDE CONCEPT

Dr. Norman Vincent Peale was the first to popularize the power of attitude in his 1952 best-selling book, *The Power of Positive Thinking*. As a child, he battled strong feelings of inferiority, and found that positive thinking turned his life around.

Studies have shown that people who develop and maintain positive attitudes and expect great things are likely to achieve them. They are happier, healthier, and more successful than people with a pessimistic view of life. Doctors have found that a positive attitude can speed a patient's recovery, strengthen resistance to disease, and help fortify the immune system. The habit of seeing the glass as half empty rather than half-full can be hazardous to your health!

WORDS . . .

A positive attitude consists of words and pictures. It is important to tell yourself your goals in order to strengthen your commitment to achieving them.

. . . AND PICTURES

In addition to telling yourself you will succeed, it is helpful to use the technique of visualization — actually *seeing* yourself in a position of success, e.g., delivering a good speech, getting a promotion, making the team or being chosen for the play — to reinforce the encouraging messages you send to yourself. Visualization has become a trusted tool in the fields of sports psychology, sales, writing, and others; it can work just as well in any arena in which you seek to succeed.

Here is a formula for working on visions of success. Try it for a while and see if it works for you. The secret is to keep at it.

I x V = R   Imagination x Visualization = Reality!

꩜

Mike: During my high school practice sessions at Cambridge Rindge & Latin, I used to take Polaroid pictures of each team member shooting a basketball with perfect form. Then I instructed that player to put the picture on his refrigerator so he could see that perfect form over and over again. It worked — the players used visualization and many improved their shooting percentages!

꩜

DEVELOPING A POSITIVE ATTITUDE

Positive attitudes in the workplace can facilitate good communication, improve teamwork, boost morale, and increase productivity — not to mention what it can do to your chances for success. A positive attitude at home can promote harmony, increase respect, and improve relationships. The net result of a positive attitude is a more fulfilling, happier life for you and those around you.

How do you develop and maintain a positive attitude, particularly when circumstances in your life become difficult? The first step is to evaluate your current attitude — how it developed, and why it developed. Is any adjustment needed? Often our current attitudes spring from events or conditions that occurred years ago or in childhood, which we have managed to push to the back of our minds.

Bringing up old memories can sometimes be painful, but if you can determine the origin of your behavior, you can change it. Conduct a self assessment with the help of friends or family who can supplement your memories and/or provide objective input and insight. When going through this process, the key point to analyze is how you responded in the past to stressful situations. Did you let anger get in the way of your progress? Or, did you decide to get moving and change things?

If the former question describes your response, it may be time for an attitude adjustment. If the latter statement is more accurate, then you agree with Sir Winston Churchill, who once remarked, "A pessimist sees the difficulty in every opportunity; an optimist sees the opportunity in every difficulty."

⭐

Mike: In my business, if I cannot find a way to control anger and frustration, I'll wind up watching the game from the locker room after being ejected. I learned this lesson the hard way when I got my first technical foul while playing for Northeastern University.

I had a bad attitude because I had been sitting on the bench for the better part of the game. I could not understand why the coach was not playing me, as I had performed very well in our previous game. Not only that, the game was against our arch rival — Boston University. To rub further salt in the wound, my girlfriend was watching from the stands, so I was missing a golden opportunity to impress her with my athletic prowess.

When I finally got into the game in the closing minutes, I was called for a foul. The foul, on top of my not playing, was the last straw. When the referee asked for the ball, he got it — right in his midsection. Of course, then I was assessed a technical foul. This made no one happy — my coach or me.

The time had come to develop some methods for keeping anger and frustration in check, for not allowing circumstances to sour my attitude. So, over the years, I came up with the following:

ANGER MANAGEMENT TIPS

- QUIETLY COUNT TO TEN BEFORE REACTING IN A STRESSFUL SITUATION.

- DON'T DO, OR SAY, ANYTHING IN ANGER THAT YOU'LL REGRET LATER.

- ATTEMPT TO FIGURE OUT THE SOURCE OF YOUR ANGER — IS IT A PERSON OR A SITUATION? (YOU MAY BE ABLE TO REASON WITH A PERSON; YOU MAY NOT BE ABLE TO CHANGE A SITUATION.)

- IF STEPS 1 THROUGH 3 DON'T WORK, FIND SOME-ONE WHO CAN HELP YOU TALK THROUGH YOUR ANGER.

POSITIVE ATTITUDE IN ACTION

Recognize what's at the core of your negative thoughts — feelings of inferiority, fear, anger, insecurity, guilt, doubt — and deal with them. To be blunt — "Get over it!" Try to be like those people you read about who battle against seemingly insurmountable odds, yet remain upbeat and convinced they will prevail.

The remarkable story of cyclist Lance Armstrong is a perfect example. Despite testicular and brain cancer, which the odds said would end his life, he survived two traumatic surgeries followed by difficult chemotherapy and rehabilitation programs. Then he went on to train for, and win, one of the world's most grueling sporting events. Armstrong won the Tour de France bicycle race (over 2,000 miles in 21 days) not once, but four years in a row, in 1999, 2000, 2001, and 2002. His is a remarkable story of how one man's positive attitude enabled him to conquer both a potentially fatal disease and a world-class field of cyclists.

We do not mean to be overly simplistic in our analysis of the value of a positive attitude in the face of difficult circumstances. But our experience has taught us that we can exert more control than we may think. The foundation of a positive attitude, when complemented by the determination to right a wrong or overcome an obstacle, can enable us to take charge of a situation and produce a beneficial outcome.

It is important to recognize that a bad attitude can undermine your entire thought process — how you remember the past, evaluate the present and think about the future. Problems in one area should not take over your whole life. For example, if a broken arm or leg restricts your physical activity, find alternative outlets, work on other things. Don't sit brooding about your misfortune. If you spend your time mourning lost opportunities, worrying about current problems, or creating future difficulties, you will never be able to take the first step to improving your frame of mind.

Mike: When a player of mine was feeling sorry for himself because a broken shooting hand was keeping him out of the action, I told him, "Why waste time complaining? Practice with your other hand and become a more complete player." The player did just that. After his recovery, he contributed more to the

team than I could have ever hoped, and experienced
quite a boost to his confidence as well.

✦

THE ANSWER IS PERSPECTIVE

Here's a scenario to consider. You go to the doctor's office for an 11:30 A.M. appointment. When you arrive, the receptionist tells you that the doctor is running thirty minutes late. How do you respond to this disruption of your carefully planned day? You can take a seat, mumble some choice words under your breath, and plaster an unpleasant look on your face. This will make all those around you edgy, and probably do a number on your blood pressure.

On the other hand, you can look at the hour as a break from an otherwise hectic schedule, and use the time to slow down a bit. Read the magazines in the doctor's office (even if they're two years old!); catch up on paperwork; make lists of things you have to do; or, if the atmosphere warrants, strike up a conversation with fellow patients in the waiting room. You never know whom you might meet that way, or what wisdom, encouragement, humor, or opportunity they might offer you. It's all in your attitude.

The key to attitude that lies in the above scenario is *perspective* — stepping back and taking a look at the event's relationship to your whole life. Should you consider the wait in the doctor's office an annoyance or should you enjoy a break in the action?

Perspective enables you to extract value from every situation. With perspective, you can see that losing a job, while painful, may not be a disaster of epic proportions, but an opportunity to get more training and an even better position. Perspective lets you consider the long-range implications of events — e.g., one loss is a small fraction of a season's worth of games.

Mike: I have learned the impact of experience and maturity on perspective. During an early, stressful tournament game as a high school coach, an old friend began my instruction in proper perspective.

In 1978, my Cambridge Rindge & Latin team was playing in a state championship semi-final game at the legendary Boston Garden. We were ranked number one in Massachusetts by virtue of remaining undefeated during the regular season. The pressures of being a first year coach expected to win a state title, plus having Celtics coach Red Auerbach and Georgetown University coach John Thompson in the stands, were intense!

Much to my displeasure, our team was down by twelve points at halftime. I was prepared to go into the locker room and express my anger in a rather unpleasant way, as was my habit in those early years. As I walked off the court, I saw my first basketball coach from the Cambridge Community Center, Rindge Jefferson, a man whom I respected greatly, standing on the ramp leading to the locker room. I stopped to greet him.

It was a blessing that I did. Rindge put his arm around me and simply said, "Mike, your kids are playing very hard, but not well. Be positive, be gentle and everything will work out." His words brought me up short, and changed my entire perspective.

When I walked into the locker room, the team was primed for a verbal explosion. What they got was a "kinder, gentler" Coach Jarvis who expressed confidence in their ability to handle any challenge. I told them to relax.

Mr. Jefferson changed my perspective and I, in turn, was able to put the game in the proper perspective for my players. It was probably one of the best half-time motivational speeches I ever delivered. We won the game, and the state championship, our first of three in a row.

⟳☆

Some people seem to maintain their perspective and positive attitude despite a life full of adversity — physical, mental, or emotional. Maintaining balance when things seem to be at their worst would be an impossible task without a positive attitude. Consider the scorecard of one of the most revered persons in the history of the United States. He:

- *Lost his mother at 9*
- *Lost his sister at 19*
- *Faced the death of a lover at 26*
- *Failed in business at 27*
- *Lost a son at 41*
- *Lost a United States Senate race at 46*
- *Failed in a Vice Presidential bid at 47*
- *Lost a United States Senate race at 49*
- *Was elected President of the United States at 51*
- *Lost a second son at 53*
- *Was murdered at 56*

The subject of this list is Abraham Lincoln, a man who suffered a number of life-shattering experiences, yet went on to become the sixteenth president of the United States and lead our country through an incredible period of turmoil — the Civil War. His unconquerable spirit and positive attitude prevented him from giving in to self-pity or quitting. He simply persevered and became a hero to our nation.

You may wish to use the following prescription to achieve a healthier perspective:

PRESCRIPTION FOR A HEALTHY PERSPECTIVE

- EVALUATE EACH SITUATION. How important is it in relation to the rest of your life?

- COUNT YOUR BLESSINGS. You have much to be grateful for — friends, family, perhaps a job, and, it is hoped, a roof over your head.

- SURROUND YOURSELF WITH POSITIVE PEOPLE.

- FACE PROBLEMS HEAD ON. Look at them as opportunities — to grow and to find more fulfilling work.

- TAKE A BREAK. Go for a walk or read a book, particularly in a tense situation.

- EXERCISE. Getting the body in shape can help relieve stress and allow you to think more clearly.

- MAINTAIN YOUR SENSE OF HUMOR. Laugh at life's absurdities; laugh at yourself. Don't take things too seriously.

Humor may be the most powerful tool for both maintaining a positive attitude and developing a balanced perspective. If you can laugh at yourself, laugh with (but never at) others, or laugh at predicaments that may seem grim, negative people or situations will seldom get you down.

In the interest of lightening our perspective, we offer some "serious" advice from a commencement address by Yogi Berra, former New York Yankee all-star catcher and manager:

- *First, never give up because it ain't over 'til it's over.*
- *Second, in the years ahead, when you come to the fork in the road, take it.*
- *Third, don't always follow the crowd. Nobody goes there anymore. It's too crowded.*
- *Fourth, stay alert. You can observe a lot by watching.*
- *Fifth, and last, remember that whatever you do in your life, 90% of it is half mental.*

If you can adopt our prescription for a healthy perspective and use it to respond to whatever life puts in your path, chances are your attitude adjustment will be a successful one. Satchel Paige, the legendary baseball pitcher, is reported to have once said, *"Work like you don't need the money, love like you've never been hurt, dance like nobody is watching."* Now that's attitude!

TALK YOURSELF UP

When you're riding on a bus or walking down a street and you see people talking to themselves, you may have a tendency to think they're a little strange, and maybe they are. But talking to yourself is one of the key methods for developing and maintaining a healthy attitude. What we say to ourselves is the biggest single factor in determining how we approach the world.

Mike: I have absolute proof that talking to yourself works. In the 2000 Big East tournament semi-final basketball game at Madison Square Garden, St. John's University went up against the University of Miami Hurricanes. Our team was down by one point with just seconds to go when one of our players, Anthony Glover, was fouled and was presented with a one and one free throw situation. (If the player makes the first foul shot, he gets to shoot a second time.) If Anthony makes both shots, we win the game.

Anthony had been a 61% foul shooter during the season — not good odds. During a Miami timeout (called by the opposing coach to psych out Glover — or to "freeze" him), I watched from the bench as Anthony talked to himself. He kept repeating, "I am going to make the free throws." He stepped up to the foul line, dropped in both foul shots, hitting "nothin' but net," and we moved on to the tournament final, where we defeated the University of Connecticut for the Big East championship. Anthony Glover talked to himself to maintain a positive attitude in a stressful situation. The result speaks for itself.

Internal conversations can be positive or negative. For example, when you tell yourself, "I know I can get this job," you set yourself up to succeed. If you say, "I'm probably going to mess up this interview," the chances are you will do just that. Try to be on the positive side of these discussions because we've learned, just like Anthony Glover, that telling yourself you will "make the shot" greatly increases your chances of success. Your words will become a self-fulfilling prophecy.

MORNING MOTTO

Expressions of your overall conviction that things will go well can be used to get each day off to the right start. For example, when you get up each morning, greet the day by saying to yourself, *"Today is going to be the best day ever!"* or *"I feel great! I'm going to take on the world!"* Such a positive statement will strengthen confidence in yourself and your abilities, as well as reflect your conviction that you will control the day's events, as best you can. These statements should be repeated often throughout the day, particularly if things are looking a little bleak. It's all about attitude!

DAILY DIALOGUES

Sometimes specific circumstances will generate an internal dialogue. When we were children faced with a hurtful situation — maybe being teased because of a physical limitation — our family usually came up with the words of reassurance that we needed to hear. How many times do you remember being told that, "Sticks and stones may break my bones, but names will never hurt me." The important message is *not* to be victimized by another's opinions.

As we grow older, we may not always have others available to us to provide comfort and counsel every time we get discouraged, so we have to replace their voice with our own. Remarks to ourselves should be guided by the principle that what happens to us is not what matters. As Charles Swindoll says, "what matters is how we respond to it." Your inner dialogue should reflect your choice *not* to be hurt or discouraged; it should strengthen your determination to meet and conquer the challenge.

⋙☆

Mike: When I was a little boy growing up in Cambridge, Massachusetts, everyone had nicknames. For the most part, nicknames were a cool way of carving out a unique niche in the crowd. However, mine was of a different sort — I was called "Crisco" (translation: fat in the can), a reflection of my rather chubby physique. It hurt to be identified in that manner, particularly at that age (I was 10 or 11 at the time), but I never let it get me down.

In fact, I used the nickname as a source of motivation; it strengthened my determination to no longer "look the part." Through hard work, increased activity, commitment and the growth process, I lost the last two letters of my alias — the "c" for chubby, and the "o" for overweight. Some of my hometown friends still call me "Cris" to this day.

⋙☆

CHOOSE CONSTRUCTIVE ACTION

Consider the following situation. You have been working very hard at your job, are cooperative and a team player, are learning all there is to know about the business, and have been told you're doing well. A promotion is coming up in your department, and you consider yourself a prime candidate, as do others. When the new job announcement is made, someone else advances. A natural first response could be: "I deserved that promotion more than he or she did." or "The head honchos must really have it in for me."

Now here is the critical point. You can wallow in self-pity and continue the negative inner dialogue *("I'm out of here!")*, or you can respond in a way that carries you beyond the circumstance. Make the following statement to yourself: "There is a reason I did not get the promotion. Something better must be coming my way." Or you can take a different approach. "I am going to work harder to make myself the best employee they have. When the next promotional opportunity comes around, I'll be as ready as I can be." In other words, choose actions over excuses.

Realistically, politics many times play a part in the promotional process; merit is not always the key criterion. But even if you are overlooked again, you have still improved yourself as well as your chances for advancement elsewhere.

Such statements are a choice of action over mental paralysis. You will come out the winner, because your efforts to broaden your knowledge and improve your performance will prepare you to move ahead when circumstances permit. (Finding a mentor to advise you at such times is important. See *Getting Along.*)

Mike: In 1977, I was an assistant basketball coach at Harvard University under then head coach Tom "Satch" Sanders, former Boston Celtics great. When he was offered an assistant coaching position with Celtics head coach Tom Heinsohn, I thought his departure would make my dream of becoming a collegiate head coach a reality. I was bitterly disappointed when it did not come to pass. My wife consoled me and told me, "Everything happens for a reason." So I swallowed my disappointment, adopted a more positive attitude and, over the next year, had one of the most productive periods of my life. My dear friend, Joe Colannino, and I organized the "Shoot Straight" basketball program to teach area youth lessons about basketball and life. I was hired as head basketball coach at Cambridge Rindge & Latin High School. There I coached Patrick Ewing, and a strong supporting cast, to three state championships. My coaching career was up and running, and it started because I adjusted my attitude after a disappointment and moved forward.

HAVE NO FEAR OF FAILURE

If you did not get the job you wanted, or the promotion you competed for, you might consider that a failure. If you and your teammates were unable to produce a winning season, you may chalk it up as a failure. When you decide that these events are failures, the danger is that you may start considering yourself to be a failure. Nothing could be more toxic to your attitude than to begin thinking there is no way you can succeed.

Take a look at the people who are considered successful — do you think they let setbacks stand in their way? Absolutely not. They analyze the failure, see what factors contributed to it, and work to control those factors in the future. They go to their "teacher" — a lawyer, a financial expert, a coach — and get extra help. They are willing to spend the time, expend the effort, and discipline themselves in order to reach their goal.

Don't let failures get you down. Think of them as setbacks, and not statements about your capability. As Albert Einstein once remarked, "In the middle of difficulty lies opportunity."

POSITIVE ATTITUDE: ANTIDOTE TO FAILURE

- PATIENCE — IT TAKES TIME TO BE A SUCCESS.
- PASSION — IF YOU ARE COMMITTED TO YOUR GOAL, NO SETBACK WILL SLOW YOU DOWN.
- POSITIVE PEOPLE — IF YOU SURROUND YOURSELF WITH THEM, THEY WILL FEED YOUR ENTHUSIASM.
- PREPARATION — LEARN EVERYTHING YOU CAN BY READING, TAKING COURSES, FINDING A MENTOR.
- POTENTIAL — WITHIN EVERY "FAILURE" IS THE POTENTIAL FOR FUTURE SUCCESS.

Mike: With regard to "failure," it is important to keep in mind that the word itself denotes finality. I try never to use the word failure; I prefer "temporary setback," "minor glitch," etc. My conviction is that it is important to experience these "setbacks" in order to grow as a human being. In the coaching profession, as in others, we are humbled on a regular basis.

For example, the 2000–2001 basketball season for the St. John's Red Storm had started with high expectations. We had two top-caliber freshmen, as well as some battle-tested veterans from the previous year's campaign. At the end of the season, our 14–15 record would seem an indication that those expectations were unmet.

I refused to let the record define our season. I chose to refer to the team's 2000–2001 journey as "not a losing season, but a learning season." This group of players had worked hard, learned much about the game, and achieved some impressive results. Seldom were they blown away by an opponent. The worst part about the season was that its early end took from the players valuable on-court, post-season experience and additional practice time. The more seasoning players get, the faster their development into a team which reacts well both physically and mentally.

The players and I regard the 2000–2001 season as the first step on the road to becoming a team that distinguishes itself by both its execution and its intelligence.

DARE TO DREAM

What are you going to do with the days that lie ahead? Sure, you have to go to work or school — but is there any purpose to your labor? The time has come to apply your newly developed positive attitude to a long-term plan. (We talk in detail about planning later — see *Work with a Plan.*) You have adjusted your attitude; now is the time to dare to dream and incorporate that dream into your life plan. Attitude is the driving force to propel you forward.

Aim high when you dream. It is possible to make your dreams a reality if you have the willingness to work hard, to acquire the necessary skills, and to adopt the attitude that "nothing can stop me now!" The history of our country is full of stories about people who have started small but created tremendous success for themselves. Homer Hickam, a poor boy from the coal mining region of West Virginia, went from creating backyard rockets to working for NASA. Jackie Joyner Kersee made the transition from the tough neighborhoods of East St. Louis to the Olympic medal stand. One of the co-founders of the DreamWorks film studio, David Geffen, went from high school dropout to record producer to movie mogul. Walt Disney is a name known everywhere, an amazing feat since he began creating his animated fantasies in his uncle's garage in California. He lived up to his belief that, "All our dreams can come true — if we have the courage to pursue them."

To create a "plan with attitude" you must approach the exercise with energy and enthusiasm. The secret is to choose a dream that excites you and will motivate you. As you grow and change in life, your dreams will change accordingly.

Mike: When I was a kid, one of my dreams was to achieve success on the basketball court. When I reached college, I modified that dream — I would become a basketball coach. Not just any basketball coach, mind you. I was going to be a Division I collegiate head basketball coach. I put everything I had into achieving that dream.

Now I have a new dream that motivates me. It is the prospect of taking the St. John's University Men's Basketball Program to a national championship and then, in true New York fashion, riding down Broadway in the biggest celebratory parade ever staged for a deserving group of college student-athletes!

However, it is not just for the players and myself that I wish a championship. Winning the title would generate such positive feelings on campus and in the metropolitan New York area. The students, alumni and fans who supported the team could take pride in such an accomplishment. The University would receive the recognition it deserves. A national championship would have an impact far beyond the basketball court; it is just such an impact the team and I work hard to produce.

Don't be afraid to aim high because, as we've discussed, failure is only a stepping stone to success, and every journey will have its ups and downs.

When we present our Skills for Life program across the country and discuss attitude, one metaphor we share is that life is like a baseball game. You have to take your turns at bat in every game. When you step into the batter's box, you may foul off a few pitches, strike out, walk, ground out, or even get beaned! But you must always get back up and stay in the game. Sooner or later you will connect and hit the ball well.

DON'T QUIT

If we were to condense the advice in this chapter into two words, they would be, "Don't quit!" An excerpt from the poem *Don't Quit,* written by Marilyn Wilson, says it better than we can:

When things go wrong as they sometimes will,
When the road you're trudging seems all uphill,
When the funds are low and the debts are high,
And you want to smile, but you have to sigh,
When care is pressing you down a bit,
Rest if you must, but don't you quit!

Success is failure turned inside out,
The silver tint of the clouds of doubt,
And you can never tell how close you are,
It may be near when it seems so far.
So stick to the fight when you are hardest hit,
It's when things seem worst that you mustn't quit!

ATTITUDE SUMMARY

We have talked about the importance of the right attitude in the approach to work, to relationships, to difficult situations, to life. Norman Vincent Peale said, "There is real magic in enthusiasm. It spells the difference between mediocrity and accomplishment." So, work, play, laugh, love, and dream with enthusiasm! The word enthusiasm has its root in the Greek word for inspired. That's what we wish for you — that each day you will be inspired to be positive and maintain a healthy perspective.

ATTITUDE REMINDERS

- EVALUATE YOUR ATTITUDE — RECOGNIZE THE BASIS FOR ANY NEGATIVE THOUGHTS AND GET POSITIVE.

- CONSIDER PERSPECTIVE — EXTRACT VALUE FROM EVERY CIRCUMSTANCE OR CHALLENGE. USE THE PRESCRIPTION FOR A HEALTHY PERSPECTIVE REGULARLY.

- TALK TO YOURSELF — IN A POSITIVE, ENCOURAGING MANNER — EVERY DAY.

- DON'T BE AFRAID OF FAILURE — TURN IT INTO A STEPPING STONE TO SUCCESS.

- BE LIKE A BASEBALL PLAYER — TAKE EVERY SWING YOU CAN.

- DARE TO DREAM.

- DO NOT QUIT.

ATTITUDE QUESTIONS

1. What words would I use to describe my attitude?

   _____

   _____

   _____

   _____

   _____

2. Write down a morning motto that will charge up my attitude each day and help me stay positive.

   _____

   _____

   _____

   _____

   _____

3. If my attitude needs adjustment, what do I need to do to make a change?

   _____

   _____

   _____

   _____

   _____

GETTING ALONG

"A LIFE IS NOT IMPORTANT EXCEPT IN THE IMPACT IT HAS ON OTHER LIVES."

— EPITAPH OF BASEBALL GREAT JACKIE ROBINSON, BROOKLYN DODGERS

SINCE VERY FEW OF US ARE SUCCESSFUL WITHOUT A SUPPORTING CAST, IT IS OBVIOUS THAT OUR ABILITY TO RELATE TO AND GET ALONG WITH OTHERS IS A KEY SKILL FOR LIFE. FROM FAMILY, TO FRIENDS, TO CO-WORKERS, TO EMPLOYERS, TO ACQUAINTANCES AND EVEN STRANGERS — HOW WE TREAT AND INTERACT WITH ONE ANOTHER WILL HAVE A PROFOUND IMPACT ON OUR ABILITY TO FUNCTION EFFECTIVELY IN LIFE, AT WORK OR AT PLAY, AS WELL AS GREATLY INFLUENCE HOW WE FEEL ABOUT OUR-SELVES.

INTERACTIONS & RELATIONSHIPS

If you are a castaway on a deserted island, there is no need to pay attention to how you interact with people. Since few of us live in such isolation, we must find ways to deal with the people — whom we may like or dislike — we come in contact with each day. All of these people will present us with a different face. Some will be kind and encouraging; some will be harsh and critical; some will be angry and mean; and some will be totally indifferent. The key is to make the interaction most beneficial for all.

Interactions carried on over an extended period of time develop into relationships. The first thing that comes to mind when talking about relationships is the Golden Rule — Do unto others as you would have them do to you. (Luke 6:31) This ageless rule is a good start and applies to all people with whom you come in contact. If you treat everyone as you would like to be treated, your reward will be a host of people who will do their best for you in return. You will experience more happiness and personal satisfaction if you take the time to develop quality relationships with other people. This takes time and energy, but it's an investment that will reap an incredible return. One has to be a friend in order to have a friend — trite but true.

It is important, then, to develop a set of guidelines for getting the most out of our daily human interactions. When dealing with others, attempt to use these simple strategies that we have found particularly useful:

PEOPLE TIPS

- **Listen.** Let the other person do their share of the talking. They will appreciate the attention and you will gain insight into what makes them tick.

- **Consider the other person's point of view.** If you can understand where a person is coming from, the journey to common ground will be much shorter.

- **Avoid arguing.** You will rarely win someone over to your point of view and, if you shoot a person's position full of holes, they may resent it and you. Respect their right to have an opposing opinion.

- **Admit when you're wrong.** Nothing defuses a potentially explosive situation more readily than admitting you made a mistake. Even if you are right, just swallow hard and find a better opportunity to make your point.

- **Kill people with kindness.** The proverb, "A drop of honey catches more flies than a gallon of vinegar." says it all. A friendly approach is the most effective way of influencing others.

Mike: One life lesson that I learned early and attempt to practice often is the one which says, "It doesn't cost anything to be nice to people." It is, and always has been, clear to me that nice guys can finish first. One such nice guy who immediately comes to mind is Mike Krzyzewski, head men's basketball coach at Duke University in North Carolina. Mike is a man who has put together an impressive winning record, including three NCAA national championships, runs a high quality program, and is already enshrined in the Basketball Hall of Fame. Yet no matter the circumstances, he always chooses to take the high road and treat people with dignity and respect.

Mike's value as a person was never more clearly evident to me than during the 1999–2000 basketball season when St. John's was involved in a dispute with the NCAA. Our point guard and leading scorer, Erick Barkley, had been declared ineligible to play in three pivotal games due to alleged violations of NCAA regulations. While officials from St. John's disagreed with the NCAA's rules interpretation in the two cases cited, the university was told that Erick's appearance on the court would result in forfeiture of the games.

In the middle of our conflict with the NCAA, we had a nationally televised game scheduled against Duke on their home court, Cameron Indoor Stadium. There was much anticipation over the game, as our previous season's meeting, at Madison Square Garden in New York, had ended in a dramatic, hard fought overtime win for Duke.

Coach Krzyzewski used the platform of the pre-

game publicity to issue a public statement in support of Erick Barkley. Few other coaches would dare to take such an action for fear of attracting unwanted NCAA attention to their own basketball programs.

Following his coach's lead, one of Duke's star players, Shane Battier, in a pre-game interview, also voiced his support for Barkley, saying, "(he) is not a bad guy. He just swapped his car with a relative and he's being vilified by the NCAA." Kryzyzewski's and Battier's sentiments were echoed by the Duke fans who gave a rousing show of support when Barkley (now reinstated) took the floor on game day. It was a thrill for all those who experienced it, and represented all that is good about sport.

I will never forget Coach K.'s gesture of support during a difficult time. Erick Barkley was also moved and wrote an open letter of thanks to Coach K. and the Duke community.

THE SPECIAL GIFT

We'd like to add an appendix to the Golden Rule — that is, try to find that "special gift" in each person you meet. Our mothers encouraged us to do this and the practice forces you to take more than a superficial look at others. Each of us has a unique talent, makes a contribution, has something to offer. If you let someone know, by your actions or tone of voice, that you feel superior to them, you will never win their support, cooperation or esteem. It is important in life always to try to MSFI — *Make Someone Feel Important* — and treat people with respect.

RESPECT

Everything we have stated about relationships can be reduced to one word — RESPECT. If you have respect for yourself as well as for those with whom you interact, the results will most likely be positive. If not, you're surely headed for trouble. You can avoid that trouble by following:

THE ETHIC OF "GETTING ALONG"

- NEVER ASK OTHERS TO DO WHAT YOU WOULD NOT DO.
- TAKE TIME TO LISTEN.
- KEEP YOUR PROMISES, LARGE OR SMALL.
- RESPECT THE IDEAS OF OTHERS.
- GIVE CREDIT WHERE CREDIT IS DUE.
- BE WILLING TO "GET YOUR HANDS DIRTY."
- HELP NEWCOMERS ADJUST AT WORK OR IN THE NEIGHBORHOOD.
- GO OUT OF YOUR WAY TO HELP OTHERS DEAL WITH PROBLEMS OR PERSONAL DIFFICULTIES.
- TREAT EVERYONE WITH DIGNITY AND COURTESY.

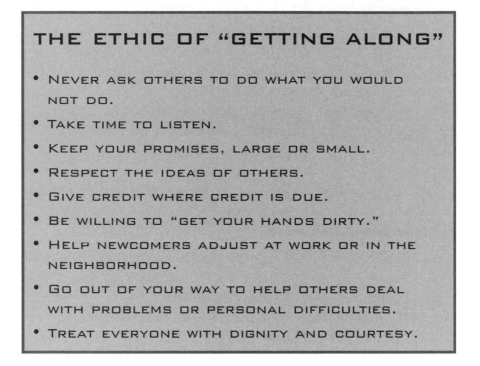

Mike: *The key point to remember about respect is that everyone has a role to play in this world. Without each person performing his or her role, the world would cease to function in an orderly way.*

For a basketball coach who calls the gymnasium

or arena his office, the building custodian becomes an important member of the team. There can be no practice if the custodian does not open the building. Injuries might be sustained if the playing surface is not carefully maintained. When I was coaching at Cambridge Rindge & Latin High School, weekend practices would have been impossible without the custodian.

There are other crucial members of the "team" who never set foot on the court — the team manager, the statistician, and the equipment manager. They help create team chemistry; I would be lost without their vital support.

Even among members of the team there are role players. For example, Jon Scheiman, whose 2002–2003 season will be his last at St. John's, has functioned as my "13th player" since he was a freshman "walk-on." Whenever another player is unable to attend practice due to illness or injury, Jon steps in to fill that player's spot. Without him, we could not run the practice scrimmages that are so important for perfecting team performance. Jon rarely gets any on-court minutes during game time, but without the dedication of our "13th man," the Red Storm would have notched fewer wins over the last few years.

So, too, in the business world it is key to learn about and appreciate the function of every person who makes it possible for you to do what you do. Companies that rely on catalogue sales, such as L.L. Bean, J. Crew or Lands' End, must respect the work of the "pickers" who fill the orders that are placed.

Direct mail firms would fail without the data entry people who provide them with their address lists.

No one part is greater than the whole, no matter what the team or organization is trying to accomplish. Mutual respect is essential in the quest for success.

⭐

WHAT YOU SAY

Treating people with respect has two facets — what you say and what you do. We return to an adage from childhood, "If you can't say something nice about someone, don't say anything at all." This maxim can be hard to follow at times, particularly in our era of mean-spirited tabloid journalism, confrontational talk shows, and trash-talking athletes. Despite changing times in our society, we stand by the above maxim and know that it will reap dividends for us throughout our lifetimes.

⭐

Mike: I have tried to discourage players from bad-mouthing or taunting opponents in every basketball program with which I have been involved. When an incident occurs during a game, I will speak to the player(s) immediately, but the heat of competition may still cause them to forget my standards temporarily. So later, to reinforce my message, I will have offending players view the game videotape so they can take an objective look at their on-court conduct. Often they are embarrassed at having made themselves look so foolish.

The same behavioral standards apply to practice

sessions. When any inappropriate conduct surfaces, practice is halted to discuss the violation. My conviction is that if the players practice with good manners, and respect the game, then those good manners will spill over into game situations and beyond.

Another tactic I use to counteract on-court rudeness by players is to have an older player, someone I know they respect, talk with the younger players, as sometimes underclassmen will respond better to advice from a person closer to their age. These veteran players will urge the younger ones to show more respect for their peers on the opposing team, the game officials, and for themselves. Better to be remembered as a scoring threat than a threat to civilized behavior.

A player's passion for the game is what drives him or her to succeed, and a coach cannot stifle that passion. But, what a coach must do is ensure that passion is focused solely on execution, not on humiliation. Again, it boils down to the Golden Rule — don't treat others in ways you would not want to be treated. Send a message. Just walk away after any effort, successful or not.

꩜

Always try to take the high road. Your family, friends and even co-workers will appreciate it, and your words will never come back to haunt you. Never indulge in idle gossip. (Someone once remarked that the grapevine is usually the *sour grapevine.* How true!) Remember, it has been said that great minds discuss ideas; average minds discuss events; small minds discuss people.

If you must offer criticism to someone, do it in a constructive rather than destructive manner, and always in private. You recall how much you appreciated it when your parents or teachers would take you aside to give you a "talking to," rather than doing it in front of your friends. Extend the same courtesy to those around you. Let them save face.

Mike: With regard to offering criticism to someone, I often remember a saying that my late mother-in-law, Lillian Hurley, used. She said, "Don't be a member of the wrecking crew; be a member of the construction team."

Take care in making promises to people, particularly if you know they will be difficult to keep. Make your promises meaningful or others will be disappointed in you and begin to doubt your sincerity and credibility. If you say you'll get back to people, get back to them. If you promise to help, then show up and be helpful. If you say you will take care of a project, then see it through, from beginning to end. Your word is your bond. When all else is stripped away, your words remain — don't let them be hollow. It is always better to under-promise and over-deliver.

WHAT YOU DO

What you do to and for people is as critical as what you say to them. This is where basic manners enter the picture. Many people complain of a lack of civility or politeness in today's world. It is up to each of us to restore a sense of responsibility for one another. Simple things really count. For instance:

THE LITTLE THINGS

- Say "Please," "Thank you," "You're welcome," or "Have a nice day" regularly — especially to people who have performed a service for you.
- Address people as "Sir" or "Ma'am" unless instructed otherwise.
- Hold the door for the person behind you.
- Offer to help someone who is struggling with a heavy load or package.
- Give up your seat on a crowded bus or train to another person, particularly an older one.
- A smile can speak volumes when you are asking for or offering help.

These small gestures just might be the only positive thing that happens to the recipients all day. And there's a double benefit — extending such kindness and respect will make you feel better, too!

Quid Pro Quo — Returning the Favor

Quid pro quo is an expression that has been used for centuries to describe the "payback" which follows an action taken on your behalf by someone else, i.e., something for something. It is an unwritten rule for dealing successfully with people, and it is important.

When people do you a favor, because they want to or because you have asked for help, they do so because they value their relationship with you. (The favor could be as significant as a lead on a job or as simple as tickets to a ball game.) You can exhibit the same appreciation by taking the earliest opportunity to return the favor.

Quid pro quo comes naturally to some; others have to work at it. It can be difficult at times, particularly if you don't have the resources to respond in kind, but to be successful in business and in life, one must understand the concept of quid pro quo and make it a regular practice.

ETIQUETTE

The expanded version of basic manners is referred to as etiquette, or the principles that society has established for acceptable behavior. The world is a far different place today, more fast-paced, more complex, and more impersonal. Such niceties as standing up when others enter the room, or excusing yourself if you either bump into or pass in front of someone, help to remind us that we're all supposed to be in this together.

There are standards of etiquette to cover more formal social interactions — business or personal. If you fail to follow these rules, others who observe your behavior may write you off as rude or ignorant. In fact, the business of teaching manners is becoming a growth industry. Some employers are insisting that their workers polish up their people skills by attending etiquette classes. Manners consultants teach them everything from the right way to enter a room to using the correct fork. Etiquette lessons have become necessary in part because of the decline in personal interaction resulting from high-tech advances or the absence of such instruction in childhood.

SOME KEY RULES OF ETIQUETTE

- **Introductions.** Introduce a younger person to an older person. Stand up when meeting someone; smile as you shake hands; look the other person in the eye.

- **Invitations.** Respond to invitations promptly and only cancel in a true emergency. Call to explain why you cannot attend.

- **Acknowledgments.** Try to send a hand-written thank you note for gifts or an occasion you enjoyed. Notes are also important if someone gave you a favorable reference, or set you up with an interview. A note of congratulations to a friend or co-worker who has done well is also appreciated.

- **Send flowers.** When you can afford it, send flowers to people who have served you well or just need a boost.

- **Promptness.** Promptness is a valued commodity in any setting. Arrive on time and be ready to begin at the stated hour.

- **Eating Out.** Good table manners set you apart. Know which silverware to use; take small bites and chew with your mouth closed; keep your elbows off the table. Don't talk with food in your mouth! And, please, know what the napkin is for and use it!

Mike: Earlier in the chapter, I mentioned a thank you note written by Erick Barkley to the Duke University community expressing his gratitude for their support at a difficult time. I would like to share the text of that note with our readers as a good example of a sincere, heartfelt thank you note.

The note was published February 29, 2000 in The Chronicle, *Duke's campus newspaper, and reads:*

"This past Saturday, I participated in a fantastic college basketball game against a great team in Cameron Indoor Stadium. Although St. John's was victorious, I believe the true winners were the fans of Duke University, who exhibited dignity and class throughout the game.

"I will never forget the sportsmanship and outpouring of goodwill shown to my teammates and me. Thanks to all of you — particularly Coach Mike Krzyzewski, Shane Battier, and the Duke team and staff — for truly defining what sport and good sportsmanship are all about."

Sincerely,
Erick Barkley

NETWORKING

As you take steps to build lasting and meaningful relationships, your circle of acquaintances can form the basis of your network. Networking is reaching out to people to obtain or share information that will be of benefit to both, as well as to offer support to one another. Trapeze artists rarely work without a net; individuals rarely do well or advance by trying to go it alone without a network.

Every person you know — from your town, your house of worship, organizations you belong to, the schools you attended, the jobs you've held — can become part of an ever-widening web of contacts. The amazing thing about building your network is that everyone in it has *their* own network, meaning you are indirectly linked to vast numbers of people. The potential is staggering. The secret is to keep building and expanding your network. Remember this key concept — when it comes to success in the world of work, *you can either network or not work!*

⟫✧

Mike: I became a believer in the value of networking when I was hired for an assistant coaching position at Harvard University in 1973. As I mentioned earlier, Satch Sanders, former Boston Celtics great, was the head coach. He had become good friends with my brother-in-law, the late Donald Taylor, through community work they had done together.

After talking with Don, I used this connection to call Satch, introduce myself, and discuss the possibility of my being hired as his assistant. Eventually, I got the job. I have no doubt that part of the reason I was hired was that someone Satch and I both knew, respected, and liked had been our reference point.

⟫✧

The sooner you make a conscious effort to build and cultivate a network, the better. There are a number of factors that make networking such a productive activity:

WHY NETWORKING GETS RESULTS

- **PEOPLE LIKE FEELING IMPORTANT.** YOUR NETWORK CONTACTS WILL BE FLATTERED THAT YOU CONTACTED THEM. PEOPLE LIKE TO BE RECOGNIZED, TO GIVE ADVICE, AND TO BE HELPFUL.

- **PEOPLE WILL HELP IF YOU ASK.** IF YOU MAKE A REQUEST OF SOMEONE, THEY WILL MOST OFTEN TRY TO HELP.

- **BIRDS OF A FEATHER.** PEOPLE TEND TO ASSOCIATE WITH OTHERS LIKE THEMSELVES, AND THEY ARE MORE LIKELY TO HELP SOMEONE THEY KNOW. IN BUSINESS, EMPLOYERS WOULD GENERALLY PREFER TO HIRE SOMEONE WITH WHOM THEY'RE FAMILIAR OR HAVE SOME CONNECTION.

- **IT'S A SMALL WORLD.** YOU ARE CLOSER TO KEY CONTACTS THAN YOU MAY THINK. EVERY TIME YOU ADD A NAME TO YOUR NETWORK, YOU ADD ALL OF THEIR CONTACTS AS WELL, ANY ONE OF WHICH MIGHT BE BENEFICIAL IN THE FUTURE.

BUILDING YOUR NETWORK

How does one go about building a network? For social purposes, just a simple address book listing friends and acquaintances will suffice. However, a more formal process should be followed to keep track of contacts who can help you in business or life. You don't have to get too fancy. A simple box of alphabetized index cards may do the trick. Or you can create a networking database on the computer or a Palm Pilot.

The information contained in your *Network Notes* should include: name, address, phone/fax/e-mail; job title/ position (if applicable) and company/organization; and a note on how you got connected. Always update the information in your notes to reflect any changes in the contact's job or personal status. Everyone who might be a valuable source of information should be on your list. Numerous contacts will be made and discarded before you end up with a solid list of potentially helpful people.

The *Network Notes* is your pipeline to good advice on job-related issues: obtaining a referral; improving your employment status; learning more about your business or industry; or gathering tips on becoming a better worker. Networking is one of the most important activities for those seeking to learn and grow as they steer their business and personal courses. Successful financier David Rockefeller has a Rolodex containing 100,000 contacts. Now that's networking!

When you find it necessary to seek out information or get advice from one of your network contacts, whether by phone or face-to-face, be organized enough not to take up too much of their time.

OPTIMIZE YOUR NETWORKING

- Have a list of questions ready in advance.
- Ask open-ended questions like, "What is the most important thing you did to prepare for your career?"
- Listen carefully to what the person says. Take away as much information as you can. Jot down notes after the conversation when everything is still fresh in your mind.

And, *always* remember to send a short note thanking them for their help.

The secret of any successful networking strategy is to keep in touch on a regular basis, not just when you need something. *If you use your network only when you are in need, it will break down before long.* People will tire quickly of a one-way relationship. (See *Quid Pro Quo,* page 63.) Show a genuine interest in your contacts, and they will continue to be there for you when you need them.

NETWORKING OPPORTUNITIES

Another effective method of improving your networking possibilities is attending business or social gatherings, conferences, or seminars. Chambers of Commerce or other local business or social groups often sponsor meetings on various topics they feel are of interest to their members, or hold events strictly for the purpose of making contacts. Businessmen and women have done this type of networking successfully for years, and appreciate its value. Trade associations, service organizations, alumni groups, and government agencies such as the Small Business Administration, also sponsor informational or networking events. Give it a try; it might be helpful.

Read the newspapers or watch for flyers advertising conferences and meetings or seminars. If the topic is appropriate, the cost affordable, and the time right, take advantage of the opportunity to learn more about your line of work, meet others who share your personal and business interests, or get a line on potential opportunities. The secret to successful networking is getting out there. Don't isolate yourself.

TIPS FOR "GETTING OUT THERE"

- PLAN OUT YOUR OBJECTIVES AND STRATEGY BEFOREHAND. DECIDE WHAT YOU WANT TO LEARN FROM THE OCCASION, AND HOW MANY NEW CONTACTS YOU WOULD LIKE TO MAKE.

- ALWAYS LOOK YOUR BEST. DRESS APPROPRIATELY AND ARM YOURSELF WITH A SMILE AND AN ENTHUSIASTIC MANNER.

- SIZE UP THE CROWD. BUT DON'T JUDGE BY APPEARANCES. TRY TO SPEAK WITH AT LEAST 10 PEOPLE WHO LOOK INTERESTING AND MIGHT POSSIBLY BE OF HELP.

- ASK QUESTIONS AND LISTEN TO THE RESPONSES. IF YOU LEARN SOMETHING, OR LIKE WHAT YOU HEAR, BE SURE TO GET THE PERSON'S CONTACT INFORMATION (NAME, AFFILIATION, PHONE, E-MAIL) SO YOU CAN CONTINUE THE DIALOGUE.

- FOLLOW UP! THE MOST IMPORTANT ASPECT OF NETWORKING IS FOLLOW UP. CALL THE PERSON WITH A QUESTION, OR TO THANK THEM FOR THEIR TIME. SEND THEM A NEWS CLIP THAT RELATES TO WHAT YOU DISCUSSED. KEEP THE CONTACT ALIVE!

Mike: In the early stages of my coaching career, I knew I had to learn more about my vocation. I sought out and attended every informational event I could afford. I wanted to learn as much as possible about the game and coaching.

One such event was a one-man clinic run by Bobby Knight, former head basketball coach at Indiana University, who presented ways to teach defense from A to Z. At the end of the clinic, I was fortunate to have about $2 in change in my pocket, because Knight was selling a book called Let's Play Defense *for $1.50. I bought that book, and its contents became part of what I refer to today as my coaching Bible. Things you learn early on that are of value can help you for a lifetime.*

Networking events can be an indispensable source of information. But you should make the most of your time while attending. Keep in mind that networking can happen anywhere — riding on a bus or plane, on the golf course, or any other type of chance meeting.

Always be open to people, because you never know when you will meet that one person who could make all the difference — be enthusiastic, be receptive, be ready!

MENTORING

Mentors are people who share their knowledge and insights with an individual to foster personal growth, life enrichment, or job advancement. Perhaps the person who suggested you read this book is a mentor!

Mentoring is what got us started with the Skills for Life Program — it is its very foundation. We wanted everyone we worked with — college students, high school students or business people — to feel good about themselves, to become inspired to reach for their dreams, and to benefit from our experience. The evidence is indisputable — those who achieve success (by their own definition) can point to one or more mentors, people who helped them along the way.

A mentor can be anyone — a teacher, a coach, a family friend, a co-worker or your boss. A mentor can teach valuable lessons on how to reach your fullest potential, make yourself better understood, and help resolve difficult situations. A mentor is someone in your corner — a non-judgmental person who will not only offer advice, but also *tell it like it is.*

Studies in communities with mentoring programs for young people demonstrate that interaction with a mentor has a positive effect on grades, on motivation to stay in school, and the ability to avoid the pitfalls — drugs, alcohol, etc. — that can derail a young life. Similar benefits — positive effect on job performance, motivation to advance, clearer focus — can be experienced by the person who seeks out a mentor to guide them through the ups and downs of their work life.

FINDING A MENTOR

If you are young and have no individuals in your life who can serve as a mentor, look to family and friends, your church, your school, or organizations such as Big Brother/Big Sister or the YMCA or YWCA. You can be more assured of getting the advice you need with a mentor than without one.

We cannot emphasize enough how important it is to find a series of mentors as you make your way through school, to the world of work, to the job position you would like to attain and throughout life. Mentors can teach you the "tricks of the trade," those tips that enable a person to do, say, or wear the right thing at the right time. They can also provide you with an objective personal evaluation — pointing out your strengths and weaknesses and giving advice on how to improve. Mentors can tell you if your dreams are realistic or help point you toward a new dream if they are not.

✸

Mike: I was very fortunate to have a series of mentors, starting early in my life, who taught me the "fundamentals" of living. I firmly believe that as we grow, we become the sum of all the caring people who have touched us throughout our lives. In my case, my mentors touched me in a special way.

From my first basketball coach, Rindge Jefferson, I learned the importance of responsibility and a good work ethic; from my Little League coach, Stretch Headley, I learned that everyone has a role; from my eighth grade teacher, Miss Virginia Key, I learned that it is important to perform at your highest possible level always.

As my coaching career began, I had two of the best mentors possible — Northeastern University basketball coach Dick Dukeshire and Harvard University coach, Satch Sanders. The wisdom these men shared with me became the foundation of my professional life.

I cannot overemphasize the importance of mentors; they affect your personal and professional development in ways that remain with you for a lifetime.

✸

A MENTORING RELATIONSHIP

The best mentoring relationship is one that involves a good deal of give and take and respect. If you have chosen a mentor wisely, he or she will take the time to get to know you in depth, and value your opinions. A good mentor allows you to make mistakes and learn from them, doesn't pretend to have all the answers, and sets high expectations for you. It is important for you to listen to the mentor, provide your slant on the guidance provided, and then agree on your course of action. Unless a bond is created, one of friendship, trust, and respect, the relationship will not bear much fruit.

Mentoring arrangements can be as loose or as structured as you both prefer. You can have a regular meeting schedule, meet only when questions or problems arise, or just stay in touch. You can write down your expectations of one another or just have them understood between you.

Time or geography may reduce the frequency of contacts with respected mentors, but they should always be people with whom you stay in touch. And when you reach the point where you feel you might have some wisdom to share with another person, make yourself available. The person you mentor will always benefit, but so will you. Mentoring helps you refine your own skills and enables you to test the value of the habits you have adopted.

Finally, becoming a mentor may change the way you look at things and provide you with a fresh perspective; as we said, mentoring works both ways. The more people you have in your network who can assist you, or whom you can help, the fuller and more meaningful your life will be. It's never too early — or late — to start.

⟫☆

Mike: I mentioned Miss Key, my eighth grade teacher, earlier in the chapter. She personifies how true it is that it is never too early to find a mentor.

Miss Key always made me feel very, very important. She also convinced me that I was intelligent.

Some of my classmates might have felt that I was the teacher's pet, and I guess I was. But, for some reason, Miss Key really liked me and I certainly had a tremendous amount of respect for her. She encouraged me to strive for excellence in academics with as much enthusiasm as I strove for excellence in athletics. In fact, she was instrumental in my receiving the first non-athletic award I had ever won. Miss Key nominated me for the John F. Burke Citizenship Award, which was given to the eighth grader who most consistently displayed good character and citizenship. I was very proud of this honor.

Miss Key urged me to take the college course when I went to high school, because she thought I had potential. However, she was alone in her belief that I could handle a college prep curriculum. At that time, Cambridge had two high schools — Cambridge Latin and Rindge Technical School. The former was for the academically oriented, and the latter for students who, in the opinion of the school administrators, were not "college material." Cambridge Latin did have a business curriculum, and Rindge Tech did have a college curriculum.

In general, students' paths were determined by the principal of their elementary school. Toward the end of eighth grade, you would meet with the principal who would "suggest" which high school was better suited to you. In those days, there were few people who would challenge an overweight, black kid from a poor neighborhood to dream of a college career. Even my wife, who at the time lived next door and attended Cambridge Latin, was advised by her principal to take the business course there — same assumptions, same lack of challenge.

Miss Key was a rare exception. She undoubtedly realized that since few black athletes were offered scholarships in that era, academics would be my only route to college. (In fact, my college coach, Coach Dukeshire, observed years later that coaches did not actively recruit African-American athletes at that time because they were afraid they would not be able to "handle them.")

Despite the fact that my principal said I should study a trade at Rindge Tech, I followed Miss Key's advice and opted for the college course. But I would never have had the courage to make that choice without her encouragement and support. She was a mentor in the truest sense of the word.

GETTING ALONG SUMMARY

To be a happy and successful person, it is most important to develop your human relations skills. We call it *getting along*. Whether in work or play, remember to make the most of, and continually work on improving, your family, social and business relationships. If we get along better in life, we will go along with far fewer bumps in the road — count on it.

GETTING ALONG REMINDERS

- Follow the "Golden Rule" — Do unto others as you would have them do unto you.
- Look for people's "special gifts" and MSFI — make someone feel important.
- "If you can't say anything nice about someone, don't say anything at all."
- Keep your promises.
- Use the suggested "people tips" daily.
- Be receptive — be ready to meet new people!
- Build a network of social and business contacts.
- Use social, business events and gatherings to make contacts.
- Find a mentor or two. When you're ready, be a mentor.

GETTING ALONG QUESTIONS

1. What can I do to make someone feel important (MSFI) regularly?

_____

_____

_____

_____

_____

2. List five to ten people with whom I can network.

_____

_____

_____

_____

_____

3. If I don't have a mentor, where might I find one? Set a time frame for making contact.

_____

_____

_____

_____

_____

SPIRITUALITY

"PEOPLE ARE LIKE STAINED-GLASS WINDOWS. THEY
SPARKLE AND SHINE WHEN THE SUN IS OUT, BUT
WHEN THE DARKNESS SETS IN, THEIR TRUE BEAUTY IS
REVEALED ONLY IF THERE IS A LIGHT FROM WITHIN."

— ELISABETH KUBLER-ROSS, M.D.,
AUTHOR OF THE WHEEL OF LIFE

IF WE DEVELOP OUR MENTAL AND PHYSICAL SKILLS
TO THEIR FULL POTENTIAL, SUCCESS STILL MAY NOT
BE GUARANTEED. WHY? BECAUSE WE MAY HAVE
IGNORED AN EXTREMELY IMPORTANT ASPECT OF OUR
HUMANITY — SPIRITUALITY. SPIRITUALITY IS NOT
ONLY ABOUT HAVING FAITH AND BEING STRONG
WHEN FACED WITH DIFFICULT SITUATIONS. IT IS
ALSO ABOUT GIVING THANKS FOR OUR SPECIAL
GIFTS AND ABOUT THE EVERYDAY PRACTICE OF
FAITH, HOPE, AND CHARITY. CHARACTER MAY
DEFINE US, BUT SPIRITUALITY GIVES US OUR ROOTS
AND ENABLES US TO EXPERIENCE AN IMPROVED
QUALITY OF LIFE.

THE THREE-PART PERSON

Writers and philosophers consistently describe the human being as having three parts: a body, a mind, and a soul. Each of us has all three parts, although in different proportions, of course.

You see someone at the gym working out for hours and hours every day and you may think, here's a person whose *physical* part might be getting more attention than the rest of him.

When you're a student cramming for exams, a business person working on an important project, or a recent graduate on the hunt for a job — and not able to exercise or do much of anything else — you may feel lousy, for you realize you are only using one part of yourself, your *mental* power.

And, when you meet people who have developed nothing beyond their minds and bodies, or may be interested only in the material aspects of life, you recognize that something is missing, that the *spiritual* aspect of their lives has been ignored. The evidence? People without a spiritual side tend to be concerned only with themselves, to be fairly self-absorbed.

The trick to living a happy and fulfilling life is to maintain the balance among these three: to have an active mind in a healthy body — and to attend to your spiritual needs as well.

Why? Because we need all three. Because the definition of what it means to be human includes all three. Because with this balance we like ourselves better, as do others, and we're happier. There's no formula for success here, but all three areas have to be tended. If you don't work out, you get out of shape and may develop health problems. If you don't use your mind, you get stale and dull. And if you don't exercise your soul or spirit, you may live a life without meaning.

DEFINING SPIRITUALITY

It's hard to pinpoint exactly what the spiritual is, for it means different things to different people. It's almost impossible to tell others how to get it and have it as part of their life. However, one of the most meaningful definitions of spirituality we have read comes from a letter a Reverend Bryant Kirkland wrote to his grandson. It was part of a feature on the crisis in values in America in the August 1, 1994 *U.S. News & World Report*. He writes that spirituality, or faith:

> . . . *helps you discover and recognize truth as you probe for it. It brings meaning and order to life's chaos. It enables you to handle success as well as hurt and humiliation.*

PUTTING THE SPIRITUAL INTO YOUR LIFE

It is a difficult task to put a spiritual element into our lives and nourish it on a regular basis. We're human; we're tempted by distractions in a society that applauds accumulation of the material things rather than the accumulation of values. Avoiding self-absorption and keeping our eyes on a goal of spirituality is a challenge. But we're going to try here to lay out some tools for doing just that.

Spirituality means believing in something beyond ourselves. It is not religion necessarily, although religion may be the most important part of it for some people. It is not even prayer or meditation, although they may be part of it as well. It is the belief in some higher power that can guide us if we let it. It means believing in something beyond ourselves, beyond our own selfish, human needs. When we do reach out for something beyond ourselves, we can find real peace and a sense of fulfillment and purpose in our lives.

Mike: Basketball is a spiritual activity. All team sports are. You have rituals of the game going on, affection building, people working together — what's more spiritual than that? Team members help you to get in touch with yourself — by encouraging you to develop your individual skill — and then to do something beyond yourself — to use that skill for the team. That is when the spiritual element takes hold.

We count on God at St. John's, we realize we're all part of the same family — the team, the university. We pray a lot as a team, during time outs, before and after a game, even during practices. I stress the fundamentals to our team, and the greatest fundamental for me is prayer.

We start each day's practice with a prayer. Often, Father Maher, our chaplain, will lead us in prayer before a game. He has a wonderful way of weaving together what we have been stressing all that week, for instance, playing better together, and not being selfish. We don't pray to win a particular game but to play well, to play to the best of our abilities and as a team.

Sometimes when things are not going well in practice, I will call everyone together at the midcourt circle — because it is the center of our world — and we will put our hands together and pray. I'll ask God to help us give up our selfish tendencies, to play our best, and to be a team.

Some of my best talks — before a game, at half-time or after the game — are inspired by words I've heard in church the previous Sunday. The word of God sticks with us, even when we don't remember the exact context. Maybe this is why some of my players call me "the Preacher."

Why don't I pray to win? Sometimes our greatest challenges — and opportunities — come when we experience that temporary setback we refer to as a loss. It's a chance to go back to the drawing board and get a fresh start.

BENEFITS OF THE SPIRITUAL DIMENSION

When we have a spiritual presence in our lives, the benefits can be enormous:

- *We feel better about ourselves.*
- *We get along better with others.*
- *Our health may improve.*
- *We have a stronger foundation.*
- *We have the strength to get through difficult times.*

Spirituality is most visible, perhaps, in times of adversity, when people are going through difficult periods of their lives and credit their faith and spirit for enabling them to survive. How did the families of the Oklahoma City bombing victims or of the teacher-astronaut Christa McAuliffe, who died in the explosion of the space shuttle *Challenger,* survive those tragedies? How does someone cope with the death of a child, or the death of anyone to whom they are close? Faith in a power greater than ourselves is one way. The grief of the loss does not disappear, but it can become part of a larger healing process.

≋☆

Mike: My mother was careful to create a spiritual foundation for me during my childhood; she insisted that the family attend church, a central element of all of our lives, regularly. And, of course, there was always Sunday School. I often went to church alone, without any prodding from my mother. My wife Connie believes that I sought the "real" father in church, as my own dad was neither a daily presence nor a positive influence during my childhood. There is probably more than a grain of truth in her assessment.

My youthful exposure to the spiritual dimension of life developed into an abiding faith in God, a heavenly father who watches over me and guides me. I learned that turning to Him in times of joy as well as times of sadness and pain can be extremely satisfying.

Never was this more apparent than at the end of my father's life. The progress of his illness was such that he was afforded some time to prepare for his death. I was able to facilitate a connection between him and my brother-in-law, the Reverend Richard Richardson, so that he could make his peace with God. In the process, my relationship with my father also reached a new level of understanding. I came to comprehend that while he and I had a stormy history during our earthly life, we can forge a new and stronger bond when we meet again.

Thus, spirituality as a healing process is a concept that is very meaningful and makes me feel good.

≋☆

Spirituality enables us to recognize that the greatest challenges and opportunities come when we achieve not success but failure. We can redefine the circumstance in a more positive way, i.e., view a tragedy as an opportunity for growth. Spirituality, for example, will prompt parents to start a scholarship program in the name of their deceased child. The parents seek more than memorializing the child; they seek to give his or her life and death some meaning.

A POWER GREATER
THAN YOURSELF

Sometime during our lives we all will experience extremely difficult emotional trauma. The terrorist attacks of September 11, 2001 — at the World Trade Center in New York City, the Pentagon in Virginia, and in rural Pennsylvania — caused such trauma on a worldwide basis. The events shook the confidence and faith not just of Americans but people of reason and goodwill everywhere. Thousands of families mourn the loss of parents, spouses, and children while thousands more grieve over friends and co-workers. Countless people are suffering economic distress as well because of destroyed businesses or the economic downturn that has resulted from the attacks. Few Americans have been untouched by the events of that day.

Material wealth, status, and intelligence were all powerless to shield people from the blows of September 11. The terrorists' assault made it clear that there are times when only faith or spirituality can act as a buffer from despair and heartbreak. Many of the victims' families are heartened by the thoughts that their loved ones are still with them in spirit and that they will meet again some day. This type of faith is what eases the devastation from which it will take years for them to recover. Belief in a power greater than oneself can help all of us survive this, or any other, difficulty that may beset us individually or collectively. There is a prayer that we know that expresses this concept more convincingly than we can.

> *Every day I need thee Lord, but this day*
> *especially, I need some extra strength to face*
> *whatever is to be.*
>
> *This day, more than any other day, I need to*
> *feel Thee near — to fortify my courage and to*
> *overcome my fear.*
>
> *By myself, I cannot meet the challenge of the*
> *hour. There are times when human creatures*
> *need a higher power — to help them bear what*
> *must be borne.*
>
> *And so, dear Lord, I pray — hold onto my*
> *trembling hand and be with me today.*

We use this example as one illustration of the practical, daily use of spirituality in a person's life. The reality is that all of us will be faced, possibly a number of times in our life, with real difficulties. How do we face losing a job, the end of a relationship, or the death of a loved one? The secret of overcoming those difficulties is to have, or find, a spiritual framework so that we have the strength to help ourselves and reach out to others. We come to believe that there is a higher power guiding our way.

🌠

Mike: I cannot recall the source of "Wishes Granted," but for me, it explains why we all have to struggle with life at times. I hope you will find this as powerful as I did. 🌠

WISHES GRANTED

I asked for Strength
   and God gave me Difficulties to make me strong.

I asked for Wisdom
   and God gave me Problems to solve.

I asked for Prosperity
   and God gave me Brain and Brawn to work.

I asked for Courage
   and God gave me Danger to overcome.

I asked for Love
   and God gave me Troubled People to help.

I asked for Favors
   and God gave me Opportunities.

I received nothing I wanted. Yet I received everything
I needed. God bless you all.

NURTURE YOUR SPIRITUAL SIDE

Spirituality buoys us in good times as well as bad. It is a satisfaction that we can only get from knowing inside ourselves that we are doing the right thing. Spirituality, in short, can give us enormous pleasure not in a financial or material way, but the good feeling that comes from living properly and from knowing we have the inner core to face whatever comes our way.

These good feelings can come in many forms: a walk through the woods on a sunny day; a few moments spent looking at the ocean; or time spent doing a good deed for someone else. All of these, as Plato said, lift us out of the confines of the human dimension, out of our self-importance, and connect us to the universe. And in doing these, we nurture our spiritual being, a being that needs to be fed on a regular basis.

COMMUNITY SERVICE

The recognition of the benefit of spiritual pursuits has prompted high schools and colleges across the country to establish community service as an integral part of the curriculum. In many states, high school students must complete a number of hours of community service as part of the graduation requirement.

Colleges are following suit. Five Boston-area college and university athletic departments have partnered with the Boston Police Department to form the Youth and Student-Athlete Collaborative. The program exposes inner city youth to college life — in both its athletic and academic dimensions — broadening these youngsters' view of what is possible for their future. It also establishes a mentor-like relationship between the student-athletes and the youngsters, giving the latter a chance to get straight answers from people not too far removed from their age group and, sometimes, their background.

The business world also recognizes the beneficial effects of community service on its employees. In the past, employee involvement in good works might have been limited to a payroll-deducted contribution to the United Way. Now when a company sponsors a charity event, like a road race for breast cancer, it encourages its employees to staff the registration desk, distribute water, or actually be one of the participants. The mental refreshment that comes from extending oneself for another's benefit brings the workers back to their workplace with renewed energy and enthusiasm. It's a win-win situation for everyone and a practical application of the virtue of charity.

⭐

Mike: My wife Connie and I have always recognized the importance of "making a difference" in our community. Doing so makes us feel good and, as a by-product, sets a good example for our children.

In 1978, we established "Shoot Straight" to enhance the recreational opportunities for grammar school children in Cambridge. The program was structured to teach the kids the fundamentals of life through the fundamentals of basketball — teamwork, fair play, being unselfish, keeping focused, etc. By using high school varsity basketball players as coaches, we were able to develop the older players' leadership skills, and impress upon the younger kids the value of a mentor.

Shortly after I assumed my head coaching duties at George Washington University in Washington, D.C., Connie read some studies linking improved academic performance to the use of school uniforms. The article asserted that students who wore uniforms tended to be more productive, more attentive, and better behaved since they were free of "brand name" distractions.

Those studies spurred us to create the "Adopt-A-School" Program. The program supplied children with school uniforms based on a sliding scale of need. Those who could afford to do so purchased uniforms for their children. Those who could not simply paid *a $5 stipend, but were required to return the uniform in good condition at the end of the school year. Money for the uniforms was supplied through our fundraising efforts. Our adopted school was the Cleveland Elementary School, run by a gifted and dedicated educator, Mrs. Annie Maher.*

Now that the St. John's community is our home, Connie has become involved with their "Bread & Life" Program, which serves Brooklyn's poor with a soup kitchen and an array of other support services. "Bread & Life" exists to restore shattered hope and human dignity.

We hope that our community service efforts have made a difference. More importantly, we are grateful for the lessons we have been taught by those with whom we have come in contact — faith, perseverance, and the dignity of the human spirit.

≈☆

TRY A GRATITUDE JOURNAL

Many of us keep journals to record our thoughts and feelings as we go through the struggles and successes of daily life. A journal can keep us in touch with where we are and, over time, can help us to see more clearly where we are going. One useful form is called a "gratitude journal." It is just a notebook or diary in which every day we record things for which we are grateful.

New people and situations will appear often, reminding us that we are thankful for a lot of different things as the days go past. A gratitude journal is a way of reminding ourselves to give daily thanks for our gifts. And it is a good reminder to ourselves of all the people who help us in our lives. Gratitude is that part of our spirituality that enables us to realize how much our success depends on forces outside ourselves.

Inclusion of spirituality in one's life is a first step toward that success, that was so eloquently defined by Ralph Waldo Emerson:

THE MEANING OF SUCCESS

To laugh often and much;

To win the respect of intelligent people and the affection of children;

To earn the appreciation of honest critics and endure the betrayal of false friends;

To appreciate beauty, to find the best in others;

To leave the world a little better, whether by a healthy child, a garden patch or a redeemed social condition;

To know even one life has breathed easier because you have lived.

This is the meaning of success.

SPIRITUALITY SUMMARY

As Elisabeth Kubler-Ross points out, to keep your light from within shining, you must pay attention to the spiritual component of the three-part person. The benefits of spirituality — a strong foundation, feeling better about yourself, and endurance in the face of hardship — can be enormous. Nurturing your spiritual side through community service and expressions of gratitude can enrich your life with a sense of fulfillment and peace.

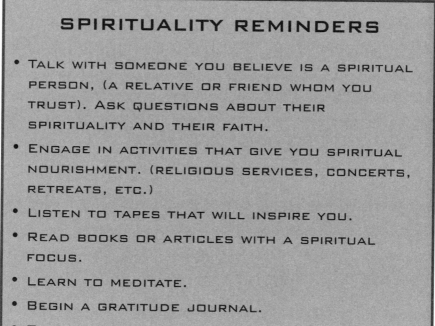

SPIRITUALITY REMINDERS

- Talk with someone you believe is a spiritual person, (a relative or friend whom you trust). Ask questions about their spirituality and their faith.
- Engage in activities that give you spiritual nourishment. (religious services, concerts, retreats, etc.)
- Listen to tapes that will inspire you.
- Read books or articles with a spiritual focus.
- Learn to meditate.
- Begin a gratitude journal.
- Find ways to help others.

SPIRITUALITY QUESTIONS

1. What activities in which I participate regularly give a sense of meaning and purpose to my life?

_____

_____

_____

_____

_____

2. How can I add a greater spiritual dimension — e.g., through meditation, reflection, prayer, etc. — to my life on a daily basis?

_____

_____

_____

_____

_____

3. How can I be of more help to others?

_____

_____

_____

_____

_____

HOW YOU LOOK

APPEARANCE AND COSTUME

"YOU WEAR A UNIFORM FOR A FOOTBALL GAME, AND
THERE'S A UNIFORM FOR CONDUCTING BUSINESS.
I REALLY BELIEVE IN THAT."

— DHANI JONES, ROOKIE, NEW YORK GIANTS

WHETHER WE INTEND TO OR NOT, WE MAKE A STATE-
MENT ABOUT OURSELVES THROUGH OUR APPEAR-
ANCE — EVERYDAY — WHETHER WORKING OR ON OUR
OWN TIME. CLOTHING CHOICES AND PERSONAL
APPEARANCE CAN SEND SIGNALS TO OTHERS ABOUT
OUR RELIABILITY, COMPETENCE, AND SENSE OF PUR-
POSE. IT SEEMS A SUPERFICIAL CRITERION, BUT
STUDIES AFFIRM THAT ONE HAS ONLY SECONDS TO
MAKE A GOOD FIRST IMPRESSION. WHEREVER YOU
GO, APPEARANCE AND CLOTHING ARE CRITICAL COM-
PONENTS OF THAT FIRST IMPRESSION AND THOSE TO
FOLLOW.

THE RIGHT IMPRESSION

Dhani Jones, a top New York Giants draft pick from the University of Michigan, was working out at Giants' stadium before training camp began in the summer of 2000. One day, the team's General Manager dropped by the weight room and asked Dhani, who was dressed in workout clothes, to come by his office and sign the contract upon which they had agreed. The young man refused, citing limited time and other pressing business as his excuses. His response worried the GM, who immediately thought there might be a problem with the terms and conditions of the contract.

As it turned out, there was no problem with the contract. The next day, Dhani Jones, smartly dressed in a blue suit and red silk tie, appeared in the GM's office, ready to sign the agreement. He stated that he considered the signing of the contract an important first career step, and one that should be accorded the proper seriousness in appearance and in conduct. He felt that workout clothes were definitely inappropriate for this occasion. It seems his parents had taught him well; he understood the importance of looking one's best. It is important to know the fundamentals of creating a positive impression:

FUNDAMENTALS OF THE RIGHT IMPRESSION

- ERECT POSTURE.
- NEATLY TRIMMED/ARRANGED HAIR.
- PLEASANT FACIAL EXPRESSION.
- CLEAN HANDS, NAILS.
- WELL-COORDINATED CLOTHING — CLEAN AND PRESSED.
- CLASSIC STYLE, SHINED SHOES.

※☆

Mike: The notion that appearance is important is one that should be instilled in all of us from childhood. Mrs. Virginia Key, my eighth grade teacher, whom I have mentioned before, impressed upon us daily the necessity of having a clean shirt for school. Similarly, when my son began to play Little League baseball, my wife took great pains to clean and press his uniform so that he could look his best for each game. To this day, my son, Mike, Jr., is always handsomely turned out and recognizes that no matter where you are, or whom you're with, appearance counts. How he looks and presents himself make me very proud.

I had even more reason to be proud when I learned that during an ESPN-televised St. John's game, Mike was described by commentators Bill Raftery and John Saunders as one of the best dressed assistant coaches in college basketball. Clearly, my son has learned to use appearance to his advantage.

※☆

GROOMING

The most stylish outfit you can buy or create will not make the impression you desire if, beneath it all, you are not well-groomed from head to toe. Starting from the top, your hair should always be clean, trimmed, and in a style that is fashionable, not trendy. In most workplaces (not *all* but most), men's hair should not touch the collar; women's hair should not exceed shoulder-length or, if longer, be worn in an updo. Your hair should not fall in your face or have to be continually pushed back. If you color your hair, use subtle shades and don't allow the roots to show.

As you "face" the world, it is best to do so clean-shaven, unless any beard or mustache you wear is neatly trimmed. (Shave twice a day, if necessary — it helps you look neat.) Women should always wear make-up corresponding to their actual skin tones to create the most natural look. When in doubt, seek the advice of a cosmetics consultant — make it clear that you're looking for daytime make-up. Regular six-month dental check-ups, and discreet use of breath fresheners, will help ensure that your smile doesn't sabotage your appearance. Personal fragrance should be applied sparingly.

Make sure that your hands are always clean, and that your nails are neatly trimmed. Women should apply clear or neutral shades of polish, not bright, gaudy colors or patterns. Polish should never be chipped.

BODY PIERCING/TATTOOS

Body piercing and tattoos have been around for centuries. Recently, however, there has been a marked escalation in their use as a form of personal expression, to "create an identity." What you do with your body is your own choice. How others may react to it is a different story — particularly for an employer/ supervisor you are trying to impress who may be of a different generation.

Before you embark on a body piercing or tattooing spree, keep in mind that altering your appearance in this way may hurt your employment chances later on, with the possible exception of the professional sports or entertainment industries. Is it fair, is it right? No, but it is a fact of life. Before you choose to do either, consider, "Would the people I want to work with look like this?"

If you have already been tattooed, or sport multiple body piercings, then discretion is key. If the tattoo or body piercing is in a location that is covered by everyday clothing, you are fortunate. If you think piercing will become an issue, it might be advisable to remove the jewelry during work hours. Tattoos can be more problematic but fortunately removal techniques are now available; removal could prove to be a very wise investment.

꩜

Mike: I can clearly recall the interview for my first teaching job. I wanted to teach at Rindge Technical High School in Cambridge and had to meet with school superintendent John Tobin. He was an institution in the city, a tough-minded, hard-nosed, intimidating individual, with a reputation for being a stickler for proper appearance.

I knew that I would have to look sharp at the interview, so I carefully selected my best shirt and tie, and paid a great deal of attention to my grooming. After much worry and final preparation, I met with Mr. Tobin, was put through my paces, and, finally, I did get the job. I am sure that my appearance, as well as what I had to say, convinced him that I was a serious candidate for the position. Appearance counts!

꩜

NUTRITION AND FITNESS

Now that you've begun to think about your exterior, it is time to attend to how you look and feel physically. Your body is the one you were dealt, but you can certainly improve on it and, most importantly, take good care of it through attention to good nutrition and commitment to an exercise program.

A certain inconsistency on the topic of nutrition exists in

our country. While information on good nutrition is readily available, the level of obesity in the United States is at an all-time high. We can only assume that people are either disinterested in good nutrition, too lackadaisical to bother to educate themselves on the topic, or addicted to "fast food." All of us have probably been in one or all of these categories at any given time. That's why it is important to become a student of what you eat.

Analyzing what you consume in a given week will surprise you. Even people who consider themselves careful about nutrition can be taken aback when reviewing what they have eaten. Junk food has a way of cropping up in the diets of even the most sensible eaters. We encourage you to chart your eating habits for several days and note what you eat and when. The results will indicate how dedicated you are to achieving a sound mind in a sound body.

Mastering the nutritional fundamentals is a pursuit that can be undertaken by you and your family as well. Here are some guidelines as to what your daily diet should include:

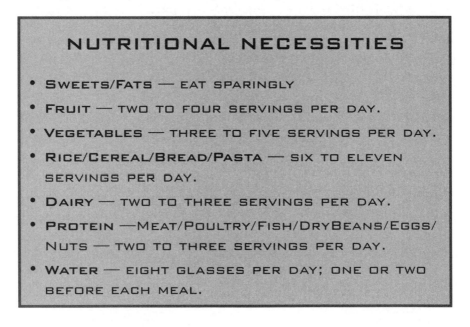

NUTRITIONAL NECESSITIES

- SWEETS/FATS — EAT SPARINGLY
- FRUIT — TWO TO FOUR SERVINGS PER DAY.
- VEGETABLES — THREE TO FIVE SERVINGS PER DAY.
- RICE/CEREAL/BREAD/PASTA — SIX TO ELEVEN SERVINGS PER DAY.
- DAIRY — TWO TO THREE SERVINGS PER DAY.
- PROTEIN —MEAT/POULTRY/FISH/DRYBEANS/EGGS/ NUTS — TWO TO THREE SERVINGS PER DAY.
- WATER — EIGHT GLASSES PER DAY; ONE OR TWO BEFORE EACH MEAL.

We have advice on what you should remove from your diet as well; we classify them as nutritional no-nos:

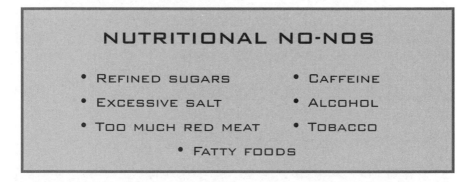

NUTRITIONAL NO-NOS

- REFINED SUGARS
- EXCESSIVE SALT
- TOO MUCH RED MEAT
- FATTY FOODS
- CAFFEINE
- ALCOHOL
- TOBACCO

The sooner you begin including the necessities and eliminating the no-nos, the sooner you'll see improvement in how you feel and in your energy level. Paying attention to nutrition now will help you avoid problems later on in life — heart disease, diabetes, high blood pressure, etc. Our last bit of advice is that you eat slowly, chew your food thoroughly, and put your fork down between bites. Taking your time is good for the digestion and can help you limit your intake, if that is necessary. Eating should be a pleasurable not frantic experience.

The benefits of regular exercise are well documented — higher energy level, reduced risk of heart, circulatory and bone problems, a greater sense of well being. We encourage everyone to set up a regular (if not structured) exercise plan and stay with it. It can do wonders for you not only physically but mentally. Here are some basic issues to consider before you get started:

Starting an Exercise Plan

If you have the resources, joining a fitness club is a great idea. They have the personnel to help you design a personal training program that works, and the equipment to carry it out. If you're on a budget, check out your local YMCA or YWCA, Boys & Girls Club, or municipal recreation department. They often have facility memberships and/or exercise and swimming programs at very reasonable rates. But do something!

If joining a club is not an option, there are plenty of ways to keep fit on your own. Start walking or running around your neighborhood, up and down the stairs at work (instead of taking the elevator), or from the farthest away parking space to the mall. To add extra "burn" to the effort, strap on some light weights. If you have errands to do within walking distance, leave the car at home. Biking is another exercise option that will reap benefits and can lead you to some lovely sights. If you have a television, tune in to one of the many exercise shows on cable channels and work out along with them. The beauty of this is that no one else will see you if you prize privacy.

Whether you prefer to exercise in solitude or with a group, make sure you do it at least three times a week and we suggest that you keep a chart. You will feel better, look better, and have more energy to give to all of your pursuits. Your mental performance will reflect your attention to your body. Don't make the mistake of those who get too wrapped up in work routines and neglect their physical well-being. Something will have to give and it will most likely be your health. Exercise is one of the most powerful stress management tools we own. It is *never* too late to begin a fitness program.

Mike: Perhaps because I have been involved with sports for most of my life, I realize the importance of fitness and conditioning. But its importance radiates far beyond just the world of athletics. We mentioned that body piercing and tattoos can be used by others as an excuse to treat you with less respect than you may deserve. The same is true if you are not in good physical condition. In our society, "thin is in." I personally don't subscribe to that notion, but I have observed the slights directed at people who may be overweight or out of shape. (It is estimated that more than 40% of Americans are overweight.)

Keeping fit enables you to sell yourself more effectively because if you take care with your body, the assumption is you will take similar care with your work. Again, it boils down to respect. If you have enough self-respect to take care of your body, others will be willing to give you the benefit of the doubt — to give you a chance to succeed. Attention to fitness also sets a good example for the younger generation.

When we are younger, playing on inter-scholastic or recreational teams (softball, soccer, basketball, hockey, etc.), it is reasonably easy to "stay with the program" and stay in shape. However, as we age, we need to concern ourselves with a more total body fitness plan. The three important areas of concentration are: strength, flexibility, and cardiovascular fitness. If your exercise program gives each of these three areas equal attention, you can remain fit for a lifetime.

Mike: My grandfather Samuel was probably the best example of a lifelong commitment to fitness that I will ever see. He did not belong to any health club — health clubs were an unknown entity in his day. He did the right thing instinctively. What "Pa" did was walk everywhere — all over the city of Cambridge. He walked every day of his life, until he died at the age of 91. The only day he ever spent in a hospital was the day he passed away. Pa didn't have an ounce of body fat and was always a snappy dresser to boot. I hope that his longevity and ability to stay active runs in the family!

DRESSING UP

For many, the confusion about proper business attire can be traced to the onset of "casual Friday" — a day on which more informal clothes became acceptable in the workplace. The problem was to determine what constituted "casual" and what constituted "inappropriate." With dot.coms no longer defining the business landscape, there has been a return to traditional business attire. In any case, Mary Lou Andre, a wardrobe management consultant quoted in the *Boston Globe* October 4, 2001 advises, "Don't ignore your visual résumé, which speaks volumes about your self-respect and professionalism."

Navigating any workplace or business wardrobe landscape can be difficult. To avoid confusion, take a look at how those in the positions you aspire to present themselves — their clothing, accessories, grooming, neatness, their "presence" — and take your cues from their style. A good rule of thumb when dressing for a job interview, or attending job-related or other social occasions such as weddings, special family affairs, etc., is to wear clothing that may seem to you slightly more formal than necessary. By dressing this way, you will make the most favorable impression.

Mike: Young people often have difficulty with the notion that appearance is often the key criterion on which judgments about them are made. Their sense of what is appropriate is often underdeveloped. They have a hard time transitioning from rolling out of bed for class to creating an advantage for themselves by paying careful attention to how they look.

Once young people (or, for that matter, any of us) realize the connection between appearance and improved chances for success, they generally adjust their standards. But then they must acquire the skill of coordinating a wardrobe that is both suitable and flattering.

It would be nice if we always looked as good as we think we do, but that is not always the case. Some of us cannot always trust our judgment on what goes well with what, or what we should wear to a specific event. I count on advice from my wife, whose taste is always flawless. If people admire the way I look, I have to give much of the credit to her.

If you do not have a similar in-house clothing mentor, then look around you to find a clothing coach, a person who can help you look your best. An objective observer can help you make good wardrobe choices and offer guidance on the best places to purchase your clothing.

Whether you are still in school, in the early stages of your work life, or your career has been evolving for a number of years, keep in mind that the neater you look, the more people will regard you as a competent worker. No matter where you work, remember the three most important rules for appearance:

RULES FOR APPEARANCE

- LOOK THE PART OF THE POSITION YOU WANT RATHER THAN THE POSITION YOU HAVE.
- BUY THE BEST CLOTHES YOU CAN AFFORD.
- DRESS ACCORDING TO YOUR WORKPLACE STANDARDS.

WORKPLACE WARDROBE

The secret to dressing for today's office environment is dressing *up*. First, you should buy clothes made of quality material. Second, the clothes should be constructed with excellent workmanship. Third, the clothes should fit well and be carefully maintained.

⭐

Mike: The "office" in which I conduct most of my business is a basketball court. One would think that in such an informal setting, less attention to attire would be required. I disagree — both for myself and for my players.

My conviction is that the players want their coach to look good, to look professional, to look as if he has it together. For that reason, I always try to dress as if each game was an important business meeting because, for me, it is. Likewise, I have my players' game uniforms fitted to them each year, with standards as to length of shorts, cut, and sizing. Nothing detracts more from a team's appearance than outlandish, ill-fitting uniforms, and I believe there is a direct correlation between how you dress and how you perform.

I only wish that the NCAA, which oversees collegiate athletics, did not consider "road" or "traveling clothes" as an "extra benefit." A team, presenting itself to the public in tailored slacks, shirt, necktie, and blazer makes a powerful statement about both its attention to detail and its seriousness of purpose and reflects well on the school it represents.

⭐

While it may seem that current office dress codes are fuzzy at best, there are still basic guidelines that should be followed if you truly want to "dress for success."

DRESSING FOR SUCCESS

- WHEN IN DOUBT, IT IS BETTER TO OVERDRESS THAN UNDERDRESS.

- YOUR WARDROBE SHOULD REFLECT SOME RESPECT NOT ONLY FOR YOURSELF BUT ALSO FOR THE SERIOUSNESS WITH WHICH YOU TAKE YOUR WORK.

- STEER CLEAR OF ACTIVE SPORTS ITEMS LIKE WIND-BREAKERS, DRAWSTRING PANTS, AND SWEATSHIRTS.

- A TWENTY-FIVE YEAR OLD CAN DRESS IN A STYLE THAT A FORTY-FIVE YEAR OLD CANNOT. A THIN PERSON CAN WEAR CLOTHING THAT A HEAVIER PERSON CANNOT. DRESS FOR YOUR AGE AND BODY TYPE.

- KEEP YOUR COLOR SELECTION SIMPLE: BLUES, GRAYS, BROWNS, AND CAMELS. THIS EASES THE PROCESS OF COORDINATION. MORE VIVID COLORS MAY BE USED AS ACCENTS.

- NEW SUITS IN YOUR WARDROBE SHOULD BE VERY VERSATILE. YOU SHOULD BE ABLE TO WEAR THE JACKET AND THE PANTS/SKIRT SEPARATELY.

- KEEP IN MIND ONE IMPORTANT FACT: YOU NEVER KNOW WHEN SOMEONE YOU NEED TO IMPRESS MIGHT SHOW UP UNANNOUNCED.

When you begin to assemble your wardrobe, or are evaluating what you already own that can be categorized as "work clothes," make sure the following classic pieces are included:

WORKPLACE WARDROBE MUST HAVES

Men

- *Navy or gray wool or wool-blend suit*
- *White dress shirt*
- *Simple patterned or striped tie*
- *Black oxford shoes*
- *Black leather belt*

Women

- *Dark colored suit, conservative style, not too trendy*
- *Off-white silk blouse*
- *Flesh-colored hosiery*
- *Black pumps, conservative height heels*

For a more relaxed work environment, be sure the following items are in your closet:

WARDROBE ADDITIONS FOR CASUAL DAYS

Men

- *All cotton or fabric blend slacks, e.g., cords, brushed cotton, wool*
- *Collared shirts in a variety of colors and patterns*
- *Sweaters or sweater vests*
- *Sport coat(s), especially a blue blazer*
- *Appropriate footwear (no athletic shoes or sandals)*

Women

- *Slacks or pantsuits or skirts*
- *Cotton blouses*
- *Sweater set*
- *Simple dark-colored dress*
- *Appropriate footwear (no athletic shoes, dress sandals only)*

How many outfits do you need for work? Not as many as you might think, provided you buy carefully and with an eye toward mixing and matching. For example, a man can be appropriately dressed for any occasion if the following items are in his closet:

Navy pinstripe suit	*Tweed sport coat*
Gray suit (wool blend)	*Three pairs of trousers*
Four shirts	*Collection of 4 sweaters —*
Three necktie	*V-neck, crew neck, cardigan,*
	and turtleneck

It might seem that three pairs of trousers are not enough but, in actuality, there are five available pairs of trousers when you consider that the suit trousers can be worn with or without their matching suit jackets. A turtleneck sweater can be worn with a sport coat for a more casual but still smart look. We do not mean to imply that a suit is no longer a requirement — it is still the best choice when an important appointment is scheduled, a presentation must be delivered, or a special after-hours business event is scheduled. Clever coordination of the above pieces of clothing can ensure the appropriate look to accommodate whatever the day's schedule includes.

The same principles apply to women's clothing — a carefully purchased, but not necessarily extensive wardrobe leaves you prepared for any occasion.

In general, high-end clothing fits better, is constructed of fabrics that are richer in color and texture, and is of a style that will last. It is better to have fewer, first-rate wardrobe items than to sacrifice quality for variety.

Clothing outlets that offer excellent quality, designer clothing at off-prices can help you create a serious impression, one of a person who is both competent and confident. Alternatively, watch for sales in major department stores. Typically, fall and winter clothes go on sale in January or February, while prices on spring and summer clothes are reduced in July or August. Pay attention to trends; watch the quality stores for sales.

THE "ELEMENTS"

Here are some specifics on the basic business wardrobe.

THE SUIT/PANT SUIT/DRESS AND JACKET

After the initial blue suit is purchased, subsequent suit purchases for men could include shades of medium gray, charcoal, or beige. For women, choices can include muted shades of blue, brown, taupe, etc. Always remember to stay within the norms of your work environment. When in doubt, being conservative works best.

THE BLOUSE/SHIRT

Women may opt for off-white, light blue, and shades of pink or beige; the color should blend well with the suit with which it will be worn. A stiff-collared or button-down style in white, off-white, or pale blue are the best choices for men's shirts. You may wear darker, patterned or striped shirts if suitable to your workplace. There is some debate whether monogrammed blouses or shirts are appropriate. We think they look distinguished, and the monogram carries an added benefit — it will be harder to lose your shirts at the dry cleaner's. It's your call.

FOOTWEAR

Many people do not consider shoes an important factor in their total "look." This is a mistake. Classically styled shoes enhance a business-like image, while high-style shoes can indicate the wearer values style over substance. In general, shoes should always be made of leather, and sticking with basic colors — black, brown, cordovan, plus navy for women — is a wise course.

Closed-toe pumps with a conservatively high heel are the best choice for women. Spiked heels are never recommended as they send the wrong message about your sense of purpose. Men should wear laced oxfords unless a more casual environment favors tasseled or patterned "loafer" type shoes.

ACCESSORIES:NECKTIES

Neckties should enhance your look, adding polish and style. Ties can make a powerful statement about your status, ability, and personality and can make you feel good about yourself. Nothing can do more damage to the image you wish to create than a tie that is ill-fitting, stained, doesn't match well, and appears inexpensive. Here is our advice on ties:

- *Choose a well constructed silk tie in a medium width.*

- *Brightness of color and boldness of pattern will depend upon where you work; vivid ties, in red or yellow, are "power ties."*

- *Use the "Two Out of Three" rule when choosing a tie to wear each day with a jacket and shirt — two patterns with one solid or two solids with one pattern.*

Solid color ties in subdued tones will always be appropriate. Your next choices could include a "rep" tie (one with diagonal stripes), a "club" tie (one with small crests, shields, or other figure), or a paisley (multi-colored and coordinates with a variety of suits). It is probably best to leave the Mickey Mouse ties at home. We cannot overemphasize how much a good-looking tie can do for your "look" — much more than an expensive suit or shirt.

HOSIERY AND SOCKS

Hosiery and socks are an accompaniment to, not a focal point of, your outfit. Here are our suggestions:

Men	Women
• *Thin dress socks in a solid color subtle pattern*	• *Panty hose (or knee-highs under slacks) at all times*
• *Match color of pants and shoes*	• *Flesh tones preferable*
• *Thicker socks for "casual" days*	• *Navy acceptable*

Accessories such as briefcases and handbags can be important for the person who wants to "dress for success."

Briefcases	Handbags
• *Shade similar to your shoes*	• *Simple, not too large*
• *Constructed of plain leather*	• *Constructed of plain leather*
• *Streamlined style*	• *Shades to match shoe color*
• *Contents well organized*	• *Contents neatly organized*

LOOK SHARP, BE SHARP: PUTTING THE PIECES TOGETHER

We consider the individual elements that make up much of the workplace wardrobe and recommended standards for fit and maintenance in the table below. These standards apply whether you work in an office, are traveling for work, or are employed at a start-up business, large or small. Look sharp, be sharp and act sharp, no matter for whom you work — your appearance may open doors and present surprising opportunities.

The standards we suggest can help anyone look his or her best and neatest every day. All of the suggestions as to fit and clothing care apply equally as well to those who are in uniformed professions, service industries, retail, etc. If you work on a construction site, you are more likely to be mistaken for the foreman if your work clothes are well maintained. By looking sharp no matter what your job, you are automatically given more respect.

BASIC APPEARANCE, FIT, AND CARE

	APPEARANCE/FIT	CARE

Suit/Sportscoat
Slacks/Skirt

Men
- Suit pants/slacks should touch the top of the shoe in front and extend over the back of the shoe without touching the ground

• Suits, sport coats and slacks should be dry cleaned and pressed regularly

Women
- Slacks should touch the top of the shoe and cover the ankle

• If dry cleaning is too costly, buy "wrinkle free" fabrics and launder at home

Men/Women
- Pant/skirt waistbands should fit naturally, neither too tight nor too loose
- Jacket sleeve should extend no farther than the bend in the wrist
- Jacket back should not bind or pull; no visible strain on front buttons
- Double-breasted jacket should always be worn buttoned
- Jackets should always be worn when meeting with the boss, a client, or anyone of importance

• Have enough suits/uniforms so that you can rotate them through a regular cleaning schedule

Shirt/Blouse

Men
- The shirt should be long enough to stay tucked in.
- Collar should be neither too tight nor too loose.
- Measure your neck and buy a shirt with a collar that is a half-size larger.
- Apply the same rule to sleeve length.

• Launder and press shirts or blouses after each wearing.

Women
- Revealing necklines are always inappropriate.
- Avoid sheer blouses.

	APPEARANCE/FIT	CARE

Shoes

Men/Women
- Shoes should be polished regularly.
- If driving your car marks up your shoes, have a pair set aside just for driving.

Soles and heels should be replaced when showing signs of wear.

Neckties

Men
- Make sure the tie is tightly knotted and extends just to the belt buckle.

Ties should always be pressed and spot-free.

Socks/Hosiery

Men/Women
- Socks should fit so that no skin shows when your legs are crossed (over-the-calf or knee-high length).

Women
- Hosiery should be worn at all times with dresses and skirts and be run free.

Belts

Men/Women
- Belts should be no more than 1 to 1 1/2 inches wide.

Jewelry

Men
- A wedding band and/or school ring, plus wristwatch, are enough.
- Do *not* wear an earring unless it's an accepted practice.

Women
- Combine a tasteful necklace, bracelet, watch, and earrings; if gold or silver, don't mix the metals.

- Limit rings to one per hand (except for engagement and wedding rings).
- Limit earrings to one per ear. It is preferable not to have them extend below the earlobe.

Men/Women
- Watches should be inconspicuous, with a thin gold, silver or leather band.

 ⟡

Mike: I really enjoy putting together all the wardrobe elements and creating a polished image. It may be that my enthusiasm for dressing up stems from my childhood. There was a reason that I earned the nickname "Crisco" as a kid. I was very overweight and had to buy my clothes in the "husky" department. Even then, my trousers would have to be reinforced with extra material because of the wear and tear my weight caused. Also, my family's financial circumstances were such that the boys had only one pair of pants to wear to school. They were washed and dried every night to be worn the next day.

As I got older, I began to slim down and my clothing choices broadened. However, price tags were still a factor. I can remember that during my first few years of coaching, I wore the same blue suit for every game. My wife had purchased it on sale at a store in Harvard Square. I certainly got my money's worth out of that suit!

Today, I would have to say that clothing may be my chief vice. The severe wardrobe limitations of my youth have given way to a passion for looking as sharp as I possibly can.

No matter how you earn a living, there are a number of skills you need to apply in the execution of your job. Each chapter of this book outlines a skill that we believe is necessary for you to succeed. It is important not to underestimate the power of costume in building your self-confidence, creating an image, and presenting yourself in the most positive manner possible.

We all want to look sharp but it is not an easy task to look as "put together" as the people we see on television or in fashion magazines. There are real people out there who look sharp everyday, however, and their secret is taking time — to decide what to wear, to make sure every wardrobe element is in top-notch shape, and to dress with deliberation. If you spend a similar amount of time, we believe you will look your best every day.

APPEARANCE AND COSTUME SUMMARY

It is always important to look your best in public — on the job, at social engagements — wherever people will size you up by how you look. Just as a good costume enhances the ability of an actor to make a character believable, the proper attire can enhance your credibility as a top performer.

APPEARANCE AND COSTUME REMINDERS

- Look the part of the position you want rather than the position you have.
- Pay attention to detail — pressed suit and shirt, shined shoes, etc. Be well-groomed at all times — hair, face, and hands.
- Optimize performance by keeping fit. Commit to a regular exercise program.
- Buy the best clothing you can afford. Shop at outlets or buy clothes on sale.
- If you can afford one suit, make it navy blue. Then follow with gray or beige.
- Purchase items in styles and colors that lend themselves to mixing and matching.
- Consider your age and body type when making clothing choices.

APPEARANCE AND COSTUME QUESTIONS

1. What areas of my appearance need work?

   _____

   _____

   _____

   _____

   _____

2. What steps can I take to develop an action plan designed to improve my overall appearance?

   _____

   _____

   _____

   _____

   _____

3. How can I make the best use of my limited funds to upgrade my wardrobe and dress better?

   _____

   _____

   _____

   _____

   _____

HOW YOU PERFORM

BASIC
COMMUNICATION

"CLEAR SPEECH IS THE FIRST LAW
OF COMMUNICATION."

— FATHER OF A. PHILIP RANDOLPH, LABOR LEADER
AND CHIEF ORGANIZER OF THE BROTHERHOOD OF
SLEEPING CAR PORTERS

COMMUNICATION BETWEEN HUMAN BEINGS HAS
EVOLVED FROM DRAWINGS ON CAVE WALLS TO TELE-
GRAPH AND TELEPHONES, FROM NEWSPAPERS TO
INSTANT MESSAGES ON THE INTERNET. HOWEVER,
THE BASICS OF EFFECTIVE COMMUNICATION REMAIN
UNCHANGED REGARDLESS OF TIME OR TECHNOLO-
GY. PROPER USE OF THE BUILDING BLOCKS OF
INTERPERSONAL COMMUNICATION — WORDS, VOICE,
TONE, EYE CONTACT, BODY LANGUAGE — STILL
DETERMINES WHETHER OR NOT THE SENDER GETS
THE MESSAGE ACROSS CLEARLY TO THE RECEIVER.
IN OUR LINES OF WORK, WE HAVE TO MAKE FULL
USE OF ALL OF THESE BUILDING BLOCKS.

THE GREETING

You have only a few seconds to make a good first impression. When you meet and greet an individual in person, over the phone or online, or through written correspondence, make the most of this opportunity to forge a solid connection. Let's explore an initial face-to-face meeting.

Begin with a good handshake. Don't offer just your fingertips but go "palm-to-palm." Use a moderately firm grip (neither too strong nor too limp), and move your hand up and down slowly, perhaps two or three times. The handshake need not last more than several seconds. As you are extending your hand, make immediate eye contact, keep your gaze steady and smile. The handshake says a lot about you at any time, but is particularly important during an interview, in a business setting, or a first-time meeting.

As you offer your hand, begin speaking. Address the person as "Sir" or "Ma'am" (Age makes no difference; we do this with some younger people we meet — it's a matter of respect.) or by name if appropriate. Add a comment such as, "It's nice to meet you," or similar greeting, and make introductions of anyone else who may be present. (*Remember to smile* because it sets the tone for everything that follows and will relax both you and the person you are greeting.)

If the handshake occurs at the beginning of a business meeting, thank the other person in advance for his or her time and attention. Close the encounter with a second handshake. If you have met the person before, add a personal touch, e.g., wish the person good luck with their new venture, or tell them to enjoy an event they will attend, etc.

✧

Mike: Adults often make judgments about young people based on how they present and carry themselves. Yet even when young people know this to be true, they often fail to look the person they are meeting directly in the eye. This non-verbal cue could be interpreted as a signal that the younger person mistrusts the older person, is disinterested, or is just ill-mannered — take your pick. What young people do not recognize is that their lack of directness could be interpreted as a sign of untrustworthiness.

Failure to look directly at those who are speaking to you can be a sign that their message is either uninteresting or unimportant to you, or is being presented poorly. As both a teacher and a coach, I immediately respond to such signals by asking the young person a question. Having to answer the question usually has the desired result — he or she looks at me to respond.

✧

THE CONVERSATION

Whether a conversation occurs at work, with friends at school, or in less formal surroundings, it is always important to make sure you are understood. Keep in mind that there are three parts to your spoken message: content, voice, and body language.

When speaking in more formal settings, try to keep the following *out of* your remarks:

CONTENT

Written communication enables the reader to take time to digest its content but it is still important to write clearly, concisely and correctly. Good writing can definitely be an acquired skill, so take every opportunity to become proficient and, when in doubt, consult one of the oldest and most respected texts on writing and grammar, Strunk and White's *The Elements of Style.* Use a thesaurus to find alternative words that convey your message and a dictionary to make sure there are no misspellings.

Oral communication, which we deal with here, is immediate and often "speaks" more to the emotions. While both forms of communication require great care, their approaches differ. When using your voice to convey a message, remember to adjust your language to the people with whom you are speaking. You cannot take back the inappropriate word or phrase; you can only hope to recover from it. Develop some care with your language — try hard to become well-spoken;

adulthood is the time to shed "cool," slang or careless expressions. We can all improve our speaking technique by observing others and remembering to *have our brain in gear before we engage our mouth!*

TIPS FOR CLEAR SPEECH

• USE LANGUAGE THE LISTENER WILL UNDERSTAND, SPEAK CLEARLY.

• SPEAK SLOWLY AND DELIBERATELY; PRONOUNCE WORDS PROPERLY.

• RELATE EACH IDEA CAREFULLY — USE PAUSES, PACE YOURSELF.

• BE ENTHUSIASTIC.

Careful construction of your verbal communication will impress your listeners with your intelligence and maturity, and will indicate that you respect them too much to use sloppy speech patterns. Clear speech will mark you as bright and competent; our society respects a good speaker.

VOICE

If your voice was the only thing people could judge you by, what would be their verdict? Do you have a pleasant, appealing voice, or one that is harsh and abrasive, or pitched too high or too low? Do you speak too quietly or too rapidly?

When you speak, use a strong, well-balanced tone without mumbling. Pace yourself properly, and those listening will assume you are a confident, capable person. Employ bad vocal habits, e.g., singsongy or excessively loud or soft tone, and listeners may tune you out. Pay attention to your vocal tone, volume, and pace so that your message isn't ignored.

Speaking too loudly can be considered aggressive and rude. Speaking too softly conveys shyness or lack of confidence. A strong tone, softened occasionally, tells listeners you are friendly as well as competent. If your voice carries a lower pitch, people tend to take you more seriously. Also, pace yourself by pausing regularly. Dorothy Leeds, in her book *PowerSpeak,* contends that people's impressions of each other are determined by three factors:

What is seen	55%
What is heard	38%
What is meant	7%
	100%

How we sound, therefore, deserves as much attention as how we look. What is seen and heard both carry substantial weight in the creation of a good impression. Your intonation (changing levels of pitch) and pace can account for successfully getting your message "heard." Observe and imitate the speech and delivery of someone like actor James Earl Jones, television anchors Tom Brokaw, Peter Jennings or Dan Rather, or the *Today Show*'s Katie Couric. These are people whose voice and presentation we enjoy, whose speaking skills we respect, and who make a living by the impression their voices create.

BODY LANGUAGE

Body language includes eye contact, facial expressions, hand gestures and posture. Awareness of all four is critical to acquiring "presence" — a sense that you are a person of substance, a leader.

Eye contact when greeting someone is important, but it is just as important to maintain eye contact during a conversation. Staring makes people uncomfortable, but if you maintain eye contact a good portion of the time you are talking with them, they will sense your interest. This gives you a better chance to persuade them with your words or just to have an enjoyable, relaxed conversation. People will trust what you say if you make frequent, direct eye contact.

We can probably sum up our thoughts on facial expression in one word: SMILE! A relaxed, pleasant smile tells people you're glad to be with them, you care about them, are interested in what they have to say, and that you are genuine. Obviously, the circumstance will dictate the use of a smile.

No one wants to converse with a statue. Be animated and use gestures both to emphasize important points and to indicate your understanding of, and involvement with, the conversation. Speech without gestures can be very uninspiring. Watch how people who use sign language convey emotion and emphasis through the use of their face, body, and hands. Adopt their animation, and your entire body will relate your message.

During a conversation, position yourself so that you face the other person squarely, signaling your full attention. When you hear something you understand or agree with, nod your head. In a more formal setting, if you have a question, raise your hand at an appropriate moment.

Finally, watch your posture as you speak. Whether you are standing or sitting, stretch to your full height, head erect and back straight — never slouch.

CONVERSATION WRAP-UP:
CONTENT, VOICE, BODY LANGUAGE

The careless conversational habits you may have developed as a youngster or teenager sometimes have a tendency to carry over into your adult/business life if you are not careful. Work hard on improving your content, voice, body language, and speaking pace to raise your conversational capabilities to the highest level possible. Take a speech class, join an acting group, listen to tapes, or pay attention to skillful conversationalists and broadcast journalists and, above all — practice, practice, practice. Improvement in this one area will reap a lifetime of benefits.

⤳☆

Mike: One of the people who most skillfully combined these three elements was former President Bill Clinton. On the few occasions when I had contact with him, I was impressed with his ability to make me feel as though I was the most important person in the world. (Good communicators can do that.)

We first met when President Clinton and his daughter, Chelsea, attended a GWU basketball game. We played U. Mass. (when they were ranked #1 in the country), and, in a thrilling game, we defeated them. The President came into the locker room, greeted the players, and made us all feel that we had granted him an extraordinary privilege by allowing him to see such an exciting event.

We met again when a GWU player, Rodney Patterson, was being honored by the American Cancer Society with its Courage Award. We expected nothing more than a two minute photo op in the

Oval Office of the White House. Instead, President Clinton spoke with me, my wife, and Rodney for some thirty minutes. In that time, his attention was focused totally on us, and he spoke knowledgeably about a topic of interest to us — basketball.

More recently, at a concert at Lincoln Center in New York, Mr. Clinton greeted us warmly and asked me to send him a St. John's schedule so he could attend some games, since he was now a New Yorker.

On each of these occasions, President Clinton's voice, words, and body language clearly communicated his interest and enthusiasm.

THE ART OF GOOD LISTENING

The average speaker talks at a rate of about 150 words per minute. Most listeners have the ability to process almost 600 words a minute. It's no wonder then that we, as listeners, can be so easily distracted. We often "hear but don't listen" — we drift, particularly if the speaker is a poor one. Moreover, there are different types of listening. For example, the way you listen to a radio is very different from the way you should be listening to directions from a supervisor or instructor.

It is important to establish the habit of being an *active listener* whether at home, in school, or in business. Doing so gives you the opportunity to acquire key information you might miss otherwise. Those who listen well, with their ears *and* their eyes, have a better chance of understanding as well as influencing others, because attentive listening makes others feel important and encourages them to listen to you in return.

Mike: Like many people, I seem to improve my listening skills as I get older — it's definitely a lifelong process. When I was younger, I had a tendency to start thinking about my reply before the people I was talking with had finished their statement. Often, I missed the key points they were trying to convey because I was too interested in my own response. I was incapable of hearing the message being sent — either directly or "between the lines."

Listening for the underlying message is so important when dealing with young people because sometimes when emotions run high, they are unwilling, or unable, to express their true feelings in a direct way. Many a misunderstanding has occurred because I did not listen with enough care.

It took me a while to realize that communication is a two way street, and that failure to listen carefully can sabotage the entire process. I continue to work at being an "active listener" because I finally came to the realization that the better I can listen, the better I can communicate.

LISTENING TECHNIQUES

The following listening techniques can be applied to a number of situations and, if followed, will demonstrate your respect for the speaker and help you remember what he or she has to say:

BE AN ACTIVE LISTENER

- **DON'T INTERRUPT.** INTERRUPTING IS EXTREMELY RUDE; IT INDICATES TO THE SPEAKER THAT YOU THINK WHAT YOU HAVE TO SAY IS MORE IMPORTANT.

- **FIGHT DISTRACTIONS.** IF YOU ARE BUSY DOING OTHER THINGS, THE SPEAKER WILL WONDER IF YOU VALUE WHAT IS BEING SAID.

- **BE OBJECTIVE.** DON'T LET AN EMOTIONAL REACTION TO THE SPEAKER'S REMARKS DEAFEN YOU TO POTENTIALLY USEFUL INFORMATION.

- **REACT TO THE MESSAGE.** MAKE EYE CONTACT AND LET YOUR FACIAL EXPRESSIONS INDICATE HOW YOU ARE RECEIVING THE REMARKS.

- **TAKE NOTES (WHEN APPLICABLE).** TAKING NOTES OCCASIONALLY WILL HELP YOU RETAIN MORE OF WHAT YOU HEAR AS WELL AS IMPRESS THE SPEAKER WITH YOUR CLOSE ATTENTION.

- **BE PATIENT.** LET THE SPEAKER FINISH A THOUGHT BEFORE YOU RESPOND. PAUSE AND THINK SO THAT THE SPEAKER KNOWS YOU UNDERSTOOD THE MESSAGE.

Remember this *listening proportion* — 4 to 1. If you listen with your 2 ears and 2 eyes, and keep your 1 mouth closed, you will put yourself in the "attention zone" and maximize your understanding.

THE PRESENTATION

Speaking in front of a group, large or small, strikes terror into the heart of many people. (For some, fear of public speaking surpasses the fear of heights, or even death!) Yet, at some point, we all must do it — when seeking a position, speaking in front of an organization, being called on in class — whenever we have to sell ourselves or present an idea. The instinct to shy away from potential embarrassment by avoiding public speaking engagements can limit our opportunities.

Some years ago, the American Management Association sent a questionnaire to over 10,000 senior executives in North America to determine the chief concerns and fears of these influential business and government leaders. As an afterthought, someone added a question to the survey regarding public speaking. Surprisingly, almost 94 percent of those responding stated that their #1 fear was public speaking and these were people of consequence who regularly spoke to a wide range of audiences.

So you are not alone if you have speaking anxiety! Although we may not often have to speak in public, we still need to learn to communicate more effectively — when answering questions in school, talking with our superiors or customers/clients, contributing an opinion at a club or civic meeting, or making a toast at a wedding or family gathering. And on those occasions when we might have to address a larger group, we need to learn the techniques which will lessen our "stage fright." We offer some suggestions below:

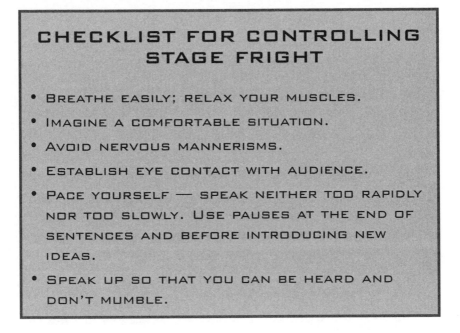

TEN COMMANDMENTS OF PUBLIC SPEAKING

So, with some slight modifications, the basic art of conversation can be transformed into the art of presentation. Through our own experiences, we have come up with what we call the *Ten Commandments of Public Speaking*. Good things come to those who can deliver a skillful speech or presentation — advancement, superior grades, the respect of family, friends, peers and superiors, and, most importantly, improved self-confidence.

I. Thou Shall Know Your Audience
Find out as much about your audience as possible — who they are, what their concerns may be.

II. Thou Shall Prepare

Do the research; find relevant examples you can use.
Organize material into simple information bites.

III. Thou Shall Always Have a Purpose

Make sure your words convey the reason for the speech
— sharing information, persuading, or inspiring.

IV. Thou Shall Create the Speech

Write and revise the speech until you're satisfied.
Pay close attention to the impact of the opening and
closing. Define what you're going to cover, cover it, and
then summarize your key points.

V. Thou Shall Practice, Practice, Practice

Deliver the speech at least five to six times out loud,
preferably in a room similar to the one in which you'll be
speaking. Use a friend or tape recorder to find out what
works and what doesn't. Know your material cold.

VI. Thou Shall Use Visual Aids

Make sure visual aids are bold, readable and simple.

VII. Thou Shall Involve the Audience

Plan for and announce that there will be a question
and answer period or ask for input during the speech.
Audiences enjoy the give and take.

VIII. Thou Shall Check Out the Room

Arrive at the location early enough to make sure
all equipment works, and become comfortable with the
surroundings.

IX. Thou Shall Deliver with Style

Pace yourself, speak slowly and with confidence. Raise your voice, gesture frequently, and use eye contact to make each listener believe you are talking directly to him or her.

X. Thou Shall Enjoy!

Have a good time — inject some humor into the proceedings. If you're enthusiastic about the presentation, your audience will be too!

Mike: My first foray into the public speaking arena occurred at my eighth grade graduation ceremony. My teacher, Mrs. Key, tapped me to give a speech entitled "All Aboard for Space" (this was the late '50s — the Sputnik era). However, given her attention to detail, and despite my reluctance and fear, I was very well prepared to deliver the speech.

My second attempt at public speaking, years later, could only be termed disastrous. While I was an assistant to Coach Dukeshire at Northeastern University, he asked if I would substitute for him as guest speaker at a local Catholic Youth Organization banquet in the fall of 1967. At twenty-two, I figured preparation and practice were overrated, (I ignored Mrs. Key's advice), so I went off to the event and expected to "wing it" successfully.

Well, I just didn't get it. I knew nothing about the audience and even less about what they were expecting to hear from me. As a result, my nerves took over and I stammered my way through an incredibly bad speech, during which I apologized often for being a poor replacement for Coach Dukeshire.

I was embarrassed and vowed I would always keep the "Ten Commandments of Public Speaking" so I would never again be unprepared for a speaking engagement.

⭐

In a survey conducted several years ago by a national speakers bureau, Bill Cosby was mentioned most often as the speaker people felt to be the most impressive. His presence and enthusiastic form of speaking, complete with gestures, facial expressions, and exceptional timing, enable him to connect with his audience. Combine the above Commandments with the tips on voice, content, and body language and you too can become a speaker that people will remember and respect!

A. Philip Randolph, whose father is quoted in the chapter introduction, was a labor organizer, champion of civil rights, and spellbinding orator. By taking his father's advice to heart, and through hard work and continuous practice, he spoke with a voice that simply could not be ignored.

If your audience's job is to listen, and your job is to speak, make sure you finish your job before the audience finishes its job.

ELECTRONIC COMMUNICATION

While face-to-face communication is always the most effective, it is not always the most practical, given time or geographic constraints. So, as we live in an electronic age, we should utilize all of the alternative communication methods it provides. Cellphones, e-mail, and voice mail are here to stay — so exploit them to your advantage and know the rules.

CELLPHONES

Cellphone use has proliferated at breakneck speed. While they certainly facilitate timely communication, their use also raises a number of etiquette and safety issues. Use cellphones with the same common sense and common courtesy that apply to all your other interactions, so they don't become a hazard and/or annoyance. Here are our rules of cellphone etiquette:

CELLPHONE ETIQUETTE

- IN A MEETING, TURN YOUR CELLPHONE OFF — NO EXCEPTIONS.

- IN A PUBLIC PLACE SUCH AS A RESTAURANT, PUT THE CELLPHONE IN VIBRATE RATHER THAN RING MODE. IF A CALL COMES IN, EXCUSE YOURSELF AND TELL THE CALLER YOU WILL RETURN THEIR CALL AT A MORE APPROPRIATE TIME.

- IN CROWDED AREAS — AIRPORTS, HALLWAYS, OR WHILE SHOPPING — KEEP YOUR VOICE DOWN SO AS NOT TO DISTURB THOSE AROUND YOU. IF NECESSARY, MOVE TO A LESS CROWDED AREA.

- IF YOU MUST MAKE OR RECEIVE CALLS WHILE WALKING, DON'T BECOME SO INVOLVED IN CONVERSATION THAT YOU BUMP INTO PEOPLE OR CAUSE SERIOUS INJURY. HANDS-FREE CELL-PHONES ARE AVAILABLE FOR CARS; THEIR USE GREATLY REDUCES THE RISK OF ACCIDENT.

Mike: Each year, my players are required to sign a contract with me that indicates their agreement to abide by certain standards of acceptable behavior. Now that cellphone use is so widespread, I had to modify the terms of the contract and include conditions for their use.

An embarrassing moment that occurred in the Notre Dame locker room made the need for new regulations perfectly clear. Bill Wennington, a McDonald's All-American, St. John's alumnus, and former member of the world champion Chicago Bulls, graciously agreed to speak to the players before we took the court against the Irish. During his remarks, the annoying ring of cellphones interrupted him three or four times. At first, he laughed and said such interruptions were common in the NBA as well. But he also indicated that NBA players are now fined for inappropriate cellphone use.

After the third or fourth disturbance, the lack of etiquette displayed by the team went beyond annoyance and became inexcusable. The incident made me very angry. As a result, an amendment to the player contract went into immediate effect. Cellphone use was prohibited in the locker room — home or away, on the team bus, and at practice sessions. People can always reach you in a true emergency; there is no need to use a cellphone when your focus should be on the task at hand

E-Mail

E-mail, because it is such an accessible and rapid mode of communication, is sometimes thought of as less formal than other means of communication. That doesn't mean that you should ignore the basic rules of letter writing:

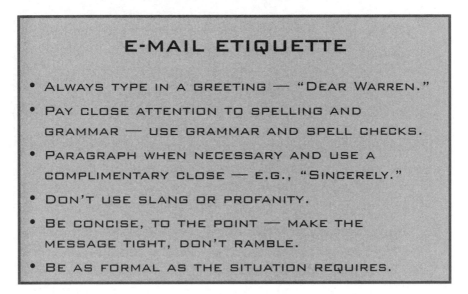

E-MAIL ETIQUETTE

- Always type in a greeting — "Dear Warren."
- Pay close attention to spelling and grammar — use grammar and spell checks.
- Paragraph when necessary and use a complimentary close — e.g., "Sincerely."
- Don't use slang or profanity.
- Be concise, to the point — make the message tight, don't ramble.
- Be as formal as the situation requires.

Telephone

Advances in electronic data transmission have been astounding, but the telephone still remains the world's main communication tool. However, it is the one we sometimes take for granted and misuse. If we failed to learn good telephone skills in childhood, our sloppy habits (e.g., not speaking clearly or with the right tone, using slang, or being impolite or abrupt) could spill over into adult or work-related phone usage. Below are techniques for developing a pleasant yet business-like phone style.

EFFECTIVE PHONE TECHNIQUES

- Before you make an important or business related call, make notes about what you want to say to keep the call focused.

- Have the right attitude — take a deep breath and smile as you are dialing.

- Speak in a calm, friendly tone of voice, and avoid the use of jargon or slang.

- If you must put a caller on hold, explain why. Don't leave a caller on hold for more than thirty seconds. If you must return the call later, make sure to do so at the agreed-upon time.

- Give your full attention to the call — don't do something else at the same time, unless it's related to the call. The person on the other end will sense your distraction. (We know that this can be a hard habit to break!)

- If you want to involve others in the room with a call, use the speakerphone, identify everyone as they speak, and raise your voice in order to be heard clearly.

Voice Mail/Answering Machines

Voice mail can be an annoying fact of modern life, particularly when it degenerates into "phone tag." Sometimes it seems as if getting through to a person instead of a machine is an impossible task. Efficient use of voice mail may reduce the irritation factor.

VOICE MAIL/ANSWERING MACHINE TIPS

- Plan your message, including requests for action and specific callback times.
- Be brief and concise; take 10 to 20 seconds at most to make your point, leave your number, and sign off.
- Enunciate clearly in a moderate tone and pleasantly (smile).
- Include your telephone number twice — the second time at the conclusion of the message. Most important — do not mumble the telephone number or recite it at the speed of light!

If you work out of your home, or have a small business, then an answering machine most likely retrieves your messages. Make sure that your outgoing message is crisp and to the point. If you work at home, resist the urge to have children record a "cute" message or to add music, or potential business callers may think twice about doing business with you. Voice messages can convey much about your level of professionalism.

Below are examples of a voice mail message and an answering machine greeting which take all of the criteria listed above into consideration:

VOICE MAIL MESSAGE

Hello Mr. Bishop, this is Mike Jarvis of St. John's University. I am calling to see if we can schedule a meeting at 2:00 P.M. on Thursday of this week at my office to discuss our team's travel needs. I can be reached today between noon and 5:00 P.M. Please give me a call to confirm at 718/555-1111. Once again, the number is (*pause*) 718/555-1111.

ANSWERING MACHINE GREETING

Good morning! You have reached Mike Jarvis and I am temporarily away. However, if, after the beep, you will leave your name, number, and a brief message, I will return your call as soon as I can. Thank you and have a great day.

BASIC COMMUNICATION SUMMARY

Effective communication is a subject that is discussed more, and acted upon less, than almost any other issue in our society. How we perform begins with basic communication. Use the reminders below to become a better communicator.

BASIC COMMUNICATION REMINDERS

- Make introductions impressive with a firm handshake and steady eye contact — be warm.
- Pay attention to the three elements of any spoken message — voice, content, and your body language.
- Show enthusiasm, vary the pitch of your voice, regulate pace, and control volume.
- During conversations, maintain eye contact and smile. Use gestures to underscore important points. Watch your posture.
- Observe broadcast media people or actors. Imitate those whose style you admire.
- Be an active listener — don't interrupt, be attentive, take notes, and be objective.
- Follow the "Ten Commandments of Public Speaking." Use the stage fright checklist to reduce the fear factor.
- Watch your phone manners — speak slowly and clearly.

BASIC COMMUNICATION QUESTIONS

1. Do I speak clearly most of the time? If not, how can I improve my oral communication skills?

   _____

   _____

   _____

   _____

   _____

2. Am I a good listener? What steps can I take to become a better listener?

   _____

   _____

   _____

   _____

3. How can I improve my phone skills?

   _____

   _____

   _____

   _____

WORK WITH
A PLAN

ALICE: WHICH WAY SHOULD I GO?

CAT: THAT DEPENDS ON WHERE YOU ARE GOING.

ALICE: I DON'T KNOW WHERE I'M GOING!

CAT: THEN IT DOESN'T MATTER WHICH WAY YOU GO!

—LEWIS CARROLL, **THROUGH THE LOOKING GLASS**

ANY TEAM THAT APPROACHES A CONTEST WITHOUT A GAME PLAN IS AS DOOMED TO FAILURE AS ANY ENTERPRISE WHICH STARTS UP WITHOUT A BUSINESS PLAN. SIMILARLY, A COACH WHO CANNOT ADJUST HIS OR HER GAME PLAN TO CHANGING CIRCUMSTANCES IS UNLIKELY TO EXPERIENCE A SUCCESSFUL OUTCOME. THE SAME IS TRUE FOR ALL OF US. DEVELOPING GOOD WORK AND PERSONAL PLANNING HABITS IS JUST AS CRUCIAL TO OUR SUCCESS. IF WE WANT TO "WIN"—DEVELOP PRODUCTIVE BUSINESS RELATIONSHIPS, REALIZE SUCCESS, ATTAIN PERSONAL SATISFACTION AND PEACE OF MIND—WE HAVE TO HAVE A PLAN.

PREPARATION AND PLANNING

If you stop to analyze successful people, you will realize they have anticipated, and taken advantage of, many of the opportunities that have come their way. If you think these people are just lucky, remember — luck is where *opportunity meets preparedness!* Think about it — people who leave things entirely to fate rarely get ahead. There are no shortcuts to success in the world of work or in life — you must prepare yourself and have a plan. The earlier you start, the better — good planning is the foundation of your future success.

⟿✫

Mike: In the spring of 2002, I was offered a supporting role in a Paramount Pictures release entitled The Perfect Score. *The film's story line revolves around a group of New Jersey high school students who must score high on the upcoming SAT test and the scheme they hatch to do so. One of the boys is a basketball "phenom" (portrayed by NBA player Darius Miles), who can either pursue a college career or go directly into the NBA.*

A scene in the movie depicts a college coach's "home visit" with the basketball star and his family. This scene is where I come in, playing myself. The producers sent me a script so I could learn my lines and be ready for filming in Vancouver during the summer.

When I received the script, I reviewed the dialogue in my scene and concluded that I didn't need to learn lines to deal with an experience that was so familiar to me. So, I didn't bother memorizing my part; I just figured I could be myself. My wife Connie badgered me to learn my part but I ignored her warnings. Finally, on the night before my departure, she sat me down and coached me until I knew the scene cold.

When I reported to the movie set, I learned that all filming that day would be devoted exclusively to the "home visit" scene. As I was the only one in the scene with a significant amount of dialogue, the day would have been a disaster if I hadn't memorized my lines. The film's director, Brian Robbins, told me that knowing one's lines is extremely important because all the actors involved take cues from each other. Only after everyone had mastered the script could they get creative and perhaps ad lib a bit. The director's advice echoed my own words, as I always tell my players to learn the basics — set plays, defenses, etc. — before they try to get creative on the court. All that creativity will be wasted if everyone doesn't know where they are supposed to be.

As I reflect on this experience, it occurred to me how many parallels it had for "real life" situations. The importance of preparation and planning applies to education, business — almost everything. Everyone has to learn their lines so that their combined efforts will achieve the desired result.

⭐

Those who like to "wing it" question the necessity of planning, thinking it stifles spontaneity and creativity. Planning gives overall direction and forces you to think ahead. It enables you to relate your efforts to your goals and gives you a means to measure your progress. Unexpected situations, problems, or circumstances that may arise don't fluster the person with a plan; they've thought out strategies to deal with the unexpected.

⟡

Mike: One day during a great 1993 basketball season at George Washington University, we were preparing for an away game against Rutgers University. In outlining our game plan, and considering possible game-ending scenarios, I had a feeling this game would come down to the final moments; I just didn't know how the action would play out. I put in a last second play that Hubie Brown had given to me at the Nike clinic. I named it the "Hubie" and we worked on it in practice, over and over again, up to and including the day before the game.

Sure enough, at the end of the game, we were down by 2 points with 1.6 seconds left on the clock, and possession of the ball under our own basket. We called the play we had practiced over and over — the "Hubie" play — made the shot, tied the game, and eventually won it in overtime. It was the beginning of our march to the NCAA Men's Basketball Tournament and ultimately to the round of "Sweet Sixteen" that year. I am a firm believer in mental preparation and contingency plans!

⟡

CREATING AN ACTION PLAN

So, armed with the knowledge that a plan is important, where do you go from here? How do you start? Determine where you are now — beginning a job or building a career, stalled in a dead-end position, thinking about starting your own business, or just trying to figure out what's next — then decide where you want to be sometime in the future. This can be the beginning of *your* action plan. Assign a time frame to your target and develop steps to help get you there. Your plan of action should take into consideration five important factors:

YOUR ACTION PLAN: WHAT TO CONSIDER

- WHAT YOU ARE DOING NOW.
- WHAT YOU WILL REALISTICALLY BE ABLE TO DO IN THE FUTURE.
- WHAT YOU'RE GOOD AT AND ENJOY DOING.
- WHAT YOU WILL DO TO ADAPT TO CHANGING CONDITIONS.
- WHAT YOUR ACTUAL CHANCES OF SUCCESS ARE (ON A SCALE OF 1–10).

SKILLS INVENTORY

We believe the first step is to conduct what we call a *Personal Skills Inventory*. This is a simple exercise in which you first figure out what you are good at (*My Strengths*), and what needs work (*My Weaknesses*). Then consider what you would like to do (*My Interests*), and how you can possibly make a living at it (*Job Opportunities*). List your own inventory of skills on a chart like the one shown below:

My Strengths	My Weaknesses	My Interests	Job Opportunities
Good Listener	*Tentative Speaker*	Sports	*Sportscaster, Agent, Sporting Goods Rep.*
Good People Skills	*Weak Writing Skills*	Teaching	*School Teacher, Corporate Trainer, Salesman*
Friendly	*Procrastination*	Music	*Production Support, Performer, Retail Sales*
Persuasive	*Scheduling/ Planning*	Computers	*Programmer, Web Site Designer, Systems Maintenance*
Hardworking	*Often Late*	Law Enforcement	*Police Officer, Federal Agent, Private Security*

Compare your strengths and weaknesses with the interests and opportunities available. Honesty in your self-assessment is key; be truthful with yourself about your good and bad points. Eliminate those opportunities for which it is clear you have no aptitude, regardless of how "glamorous" they might seem. For example, if your writing skills are weak, then a career as a newspaper reporter is probably not an option. Remember, however, that we are all works in progress and a concentrated effort on improving some skills might make a desired job or profession accessible someday.

After completing your skills inventory, make a list of contacts who can help you move forward. These are people you respect and believe can give you proper introductions and/or insights into the world beyond your current boundaries. Then prepare a brief statement (one paragraph, with date) about where you're headed.

⭒

Mike: I started my college basketball career thinking that I knew how to play, that I was going to be a "hotshot" player at Northeastern University. After all, hadn't my high school team won the state championship? I had to sit out my first year because I had transferred from a junior college. Then I barely made the team in my sophomore year, and sat on the bench, hardly ever getting a chance to play. At the end of my sophomore year, out of frustration and anger, I quit the basketball team.

Instead of playing basketball, I worked at my brother's fish 'n' chips store in Cambridge cooking fried food (and I had the burn marks to prove it). It was then that I realized that just playing ball wasn't the real reason that I missed basketball. It was all the other lessons, experiences, and interactions that I missed more than anything. I went back to Coach Dukeshire at the end of the school year and begged him for another opportunity to try out for the team the following year. He granted it and I made the team.

It was at that point in my life that I decided I wasn't ever going to be a professional player or, for that matter, a good college player. I wasn't talented enough. But I did want to be around basketball and, more particularly, be a coach. Not only did I want to coach, I wanted to go back to my high school and ensure that the next set of Mike Jarvises would be better prepared. Then, when my players went to college and tried out for the basketball team, they would have a fighting chance to make the grade, contribute, and feel that they had lived up to their potential.

Had I not been truthful with myself about my abilities at the start of that season (done my own self-assessment), I might never have realized that coaching was my true calling and passion. From that moment on I recorded everything that happened in our daily practices in a blue 3-ring binder. I described the drills, the way Coach Dukeshire taught them and how he handled different situations and people. I was beginning my coaching career. (I still use that blue notebook to this day!)

SETTING GOALS

Once your self-assessment has generated some ideas, it is time to take a look at a possible job path — choose a career/direction, or reassess where you are now and figure out where you want to go from here. (At this stage in the process, it is always helpful to sit down with someone to share your thoughts, someone who can give you objective feedback as to whether your ideas make sense. We all need good sounding boards — maybe a mentor.)

Set down your goals in writing and make them specific and realistic. They should be something that you are willing to work hard to accomplish within the time frame you establish. Take your personal value system as well as your interests into account when you choose your goals. For example, when considering a job, make sure you're comfortable with the organization's mission.

⟫☆

Mike: My coaching philosophy has always been that the coach is first a teacher. Coaches must teach the value of hard work and team play, winning with grace and losing with perspective, and making the most of one's abilities. Even though economics is the engine propelling many college basketball programs, those who not only coach, but teach, must resist allowing money to become their driving force. I had to remind myself about this philosophy in recent years when I was under consideration for the head coaching position of the Washington Wizards, the NBA team managed by Michael Jordan.

My first exposure to Michael was as coach of the East Squad at the 1981 McDonald's All-America Game in Wichita, Kansas. I remember coming back to tell my high school players that they would soon be hearing more from this talented young man. His will to win and determination always to finish first, even in practice, were extraordinary. These traits, and his native ability, enabled him to become arguably the greatest basketball player of all time.

Needless to say, being approached by Jordan, a basketball icon, to coach the Wizards was a very exciting experience. The opportunity to coach at the professional level is one that is offered to very few, and I had to give it careful consideration. On the plus side, signing with the Wizards would mean a return to the Washington, D.C. area, where Connie and I could be closer to our daughter, Dana. And, of course, reaching the very top level of one's profession is a reward that is hard to resist.

On the minus side, I had calculated a salary figure that I felt would justify such a huge, risky move to the NBA. The offer the Wizards made did not match the number I had in mind. However, beyond the financial considerations, I did think about how exciting it would be to apply my life and coaching experience to the game's professional level.

If I proved to be successful, then perhaps I might have silenced the cynics who claim that while you can give NBA players a game plan, you cannot give them advice on a life plan. The cynics would say that young athletes being paid astronomical salaries would turn a deaf ear to instruction on values and issues of character. What a challenge it would have been to bring Skills for Life along with me to the NBA and prove the cynics wrong!

Bottom line: I turned down the position. Many people told me I was crazy. And, to tell the truth, if the right dollar amount had been offered, I cannot say with certainty that I would have made the same decision. But I am comfortable with having declined and, looking back, know it was the right decision.

Commit to your goal by choosing a definite course of action *(your action plan)* while you work to improve yourself. Gather all the data necessary — your *Skills Inventory* and any other information that will help you evaluate whether the job category you've chosen represents a good fit. Find out the educational, training and/or apprenticeship requirements of your selected endeavor. When your research is complete, list the specific skills in your action plan that need to be acquired and perfected. These are your objectives, the steps toward your goal that you will need to complete within a specific time period. Your objectives should be:

- *Specific and precise*
- *Flexible (allow for the unexpected)*
- *Easy to follow*
- *Evaluated on a regular basis*

Even if you are still in school and uncertain about your future, you can still select goals and objectives and get a head start on upgrading your skills. For example, you could set a goal for yourself of attending a post-high school program or graduate school. Then you could choose objectives such as: taking the courses that will qualify you for admission; examining scholarship opportunities; learning what kind of student the school or program wants to attract; seeking the advice of a guidance counselor; visiting campuses; and setting a schedule for taking the necessary admission or standardized tests. Leave as little as possible to chance.

Mike: Setting goals and objectives are the "fundamentals" of planning. Attempting to execute a life plan without them may lead to occasional successes but, in general, an approach which is not carefully thought out will yield disappointing results.

For this reason, I am absolutely adamant about planning and stressing the "fundamentals" with my players. My high school coach, Ed Culhane, had a freewheeling approach to the game. He wanted us to enjoy our high school basketball careers and told us to "get out there and play." I am grateful that Coach Culhane gave me the opportunity to play and taught me to love the game experience; it was fun playing for him. When I got to college, I learned that my raw basketball skills needed refinement — I needed to hone my knowledge of the game's fundamentals. (My lack of this knowledge was one of the reasons I was unprepared to play at the collegiate level. A certain scarcity of talent may have been another reason!)

When I decided to become a student of coaching, and began observing Coach Dukeshire at Northeastern in more detail, I realized that the secret of his success was how well he communicated to his players the importance of the fundamentals — dribbling, passing, shooting, free throws. My blue notebook quickly was filled with the routines he used to drill the fundamentals into his players.

The current emphasis in basketball has strayed from basing success on the fundamentals. That is not to say that there aren't some incredibly talented *young athletes playing today. However, their true value is not their skill but their ability to incorporate that skill into a team effort. This can only be done if they "know" the game, and execute the fundamentals. Their light may shine brightly for a time but, without a strong foundation, long term success will be achieved neither by them nor their teams.*

I deviated from this philosophy in preparing my team for the Coaches' Cancer Tournament at Madison Square Garden in November 2000, the kick off of the St. John's 2000–2001 season, and it cost us. Our first game was against a perennial power-house — the University of Kentucky. Instead of holding practices that started with the fundamentals, I concentrated only on the opponent. While we were able to defeat Kentucky, we were defeated in our next game against the University of Kansas.

I apologized to my players for not sticking to my game plan, for not taking their preparation one step at a time. I asked for their support and cooperation in getting back to the fundamentals. They agreed and, once they got the immediate reinforcement that comes from a well-planned approach, they understood the connection between mastering the fundamentals and the quest for success.

When I am asked what the secret of success is, I reply that I have rarely strayed from the advice of Coach Dukeshire — start as if you know nothing.

An Action Plan Example

Here is an illustration of choosing a goal and then setting objectives. Let's say you are an entry-level employee who wants to learn more and get promoted. You set a goal to move beyond entry-level within one year, achieve middle management status within five years, and join the executive ranks within eight years, and, finally, become an owner of the company! Pretty ambitious, but doable. These are specific, realistic goals (you hope). Now define your objectives and set everything down, perhaps as follows:

Goals	Objectives
Entry Level *(for one year)*	• *Learn the business, ask questions* • *Learn how to work on a team* • *Watch others you work with, at your level and above* • *Study customers in detail* • *Cultivate relationships* • *Work on communication skills* • *Start networking/find a mentor*
Middle Management *(in five years)*	• *Learn how managers motivate* • *Study how to allocate work time* • *Learn about management styles and how people react to them* • *Pay attention to the "politics" of the organization* • *Work on communication skills* • *Understand the importance of costs and budgets* • *Meet commitments, add value, get things done*

Executive	• *Refine technical skills*
(in eight years)	• *Enhance planning skills*
	• *Work on communication skills*
	• *Know how to delegate*
	• *Think "out of the box"*
	• *Think "bottom line"*
	• *Perfect presentation skills*

You may think that this sounds like a lot of work — it is! Someone once said that the dictionary is the only place where you'll find success *before* work. A little luck along the way might also help. Return to your journal from time to time and you might be amazed at what you've learned about yourself and your surroundings.

⇒☆

Mike: In my junior year in college I had the goal to become a basketball coach. By majoring in physical education, I had luckily taken the proper first step.

I knew that I would have to begin a coaching career in high school because there were fewer than a handful of African-American collegiate coaches in the country at the time. So step one would be completing a physical education major, step two would be acquiring a high school teaching position, and step three would be applying for and obtaining a position as a basketball coach.

I followed a process much like the one described above (although I didn't think about it in those terms). As part of the Northeastern University cooperative program, I student taught at Newton North High School. The next year, Al Fortune (who later became principal of Newton North) gave me my first paid coaching position for the sophomore class basketball team. Positions as assistant coach, first at Northeastern and then at Harvard, followed. Next, I made the transition to head coach, first at Cambridge Rindge & Latin High School and then at the collegiate level at Boston University, George Washington University, and now at St. John's University.

It's been a long and sometimes difficult journey, but I stuck to my goal, learned as much as I could about my profession, improved my listening skills, worked hard, made adjustments as I went along, and attempted to accomplish my objectives at each stop on the way. I am in the middle of a wonderful career doing what I love. Certainly luck may have played a part but, without a plan, I would not have been able to take advantage of the opportunities that came my way. In a quote from Through the Looking Glass, *Alice asked the Cheshire Cat where she should go. He said, "It depends on where you're going." I think I always knew where I was going.*

PLAN YOUR LIFE,
NOT JUST YOUR WORK

Your work life is not the only arena in which you should have a game plan. It is helpful to take the same thoughtful approach to planning in every aspect of your life. As we mentioned in the *Spirituality* chapter, the human being comprises a body, mind and soul. Planning allows you to achieve something we all need — the proper balance among those elements. Here are some examples:

Category	Goal
Health	• *Jog/walk 3 or 4 times a week* • *Achieve your ideal weight* • *Join a health club* • *Get annual check-ups* • *Laugh a lot*
Personal	• *Get organized, make daily lists* • *Establish a savings/retirement fund* • *Look into life insurance* • *Start a monthly budget* • *Learn more about something that interests you* • *Read more* • *Laugh a lot*
Community Volunteer	• *Help people less fortunate than you* • *Join a local government committee* • *Smile at strangers* • *Laugh a lot*

Whether planning life or work, be specific, review your goals regularly, update as necessary, and take pride in your efforts.

TIME MANAGEMENT

The planning process must be monitored regularly. It is pointless to chart a course and then fail to check whether you're making progress toward your destination. The best way we've found to keep track and stay on track is to use time management techniques to help stay focused on what we're doing on a daily basis. It is very easy to become distracted during a work day or during any span of time; it is best to at least try to follow a schedule. For some, this is not an easy task. To get a good start, try to keep as careful track of time as you do of money — time is the currency which will eventually enable you to "purchase" your goals and its careful management will pay dividends throughout your lifetime.

Mike: Over the years, through trial and error, I have developed, and continue to modify, a system for bringing out the best in most of my players through effective practice schedules. Practice sessions I have run at every level of coaching follow a similar plan — a portion devoted to conditioning, a portion devoted to the "fundamentals," and a portion devoted to scrimmaging — focusing on the team as a unit. I call this my "practice plan."

The practice schedules are discussed both at the start of each week as well as each day with the staff. Thus, the coaches know what will be worked on for the week and have a daily practice breakdown. The daily and weekly plans reduce explanation time. We can get right to work.

Of course, there is an element of flexibility built into the plan. Something might have happened in a recent game which will indicate that more work is needed in a particular area — passing, free throw shooting, offensive rebounding, etc. Or perfecting a certain skill may take a little longer than anticipated. So we adjust the practice time a little bit to respond to the need. I am convinced that the ability to succeed is directly connected to one's ability to use and manage time wisely, whether in my business or yours.

I often tell my players, "Learn how to prepare; that's how you learn to play." Planning helps them to play smart, play hard, and play together.

⮑☆

THE 80/20 RULE

It is said that 80 percent of the value of the day is produced by 20 percent of the activity. It is a disturbing idea — that only 20 percent of what we do each day produces substantial results. What's happening to the rest of our time? How can we improve the ratio of time spent to what we achieve? How can you focus on results, not just on being busy? The answer is managing our time.

Time management affords you the opportunity to determine which of those activities you undertake are important and which can be eliminated. You can prioritize — rank the tasks you must complete in their order of importance. Managing time means using it in the most effective way possible, thus increasing your productivity. This is an especially important discipline for those just out of school or out of the military who no longer have an external structure to help maintain focus. We call it being "institutionalized" — being directed and/or scheduled regularly by others — parents, teachers, coaches, officers.

Eliminating distractions and making more efficient use of your time will help you meet deadlines and increase your control over each day. (Employers frequently remark that employees who are "going somewhere" know how to "manage their time.") Skillful time management will also give you more time to relax and do the things you enjoy, or would like to pursue on a more regular basis.

Developing an Activity Log

To determine whether or not you are making good use of your time, keep an activity log for a few days. (Don't try to become an efficiency expert when you try this; just go through a set number of days as you normally would!) Make note of the things you do, when you do them, and how much time each activity takes. Also comment on how you approach the task — with energy, with little enthusiasm, with dread, etc.

Once you have filled in the log for a number of days, review it and analyze the results. See how your time could be better organized and what tasks you might postpone until later. Pinpoint where time is being wasted on non-productive, low priority tasks. Successful people who have done this analysis do the difficult tasks (e.g., making unpleasant phone calls) first every day. They don't allow procrastination to create undue pressure; after they have addressed the more difficult tasks, they are free to make the most of the remainder of their day.

Mike: In the summer of 2001, I accompanied a team of college all-star basketball players — New York City Hoops — on a trip to Greece. The team was scheduled to play a number of games against international teams. The young men and I had a great time.

Travel often changes one's perspective, and on the long flight home I had plenty of time for reflection. I thought about how I might get my players at St. John's to focus on the upcoming season, how I could make it a truly productive season for all of us.

I found the answer in jet lag. While I was on

Greek time, I became accustomed to waking up far earlier in the morning than was usual for me. I soon realized how much I could get done in those early morning hours, what a productive time of day I had been missing. That gave me an answer to my concern about getting the team prepared.

What I realized is that, from time to time, we have to make adjustments in the way we utilize time in order to get the most done. If I could change from a "night person" and make full use of early morning and daytime hours, then perhaps my players could be similarly inspired to analyze how they used their time. Together we could become a most efficient unit!

⟫☆

CREATING SCHEDULES — MONTHLY, WEEKLY, DAILY

Now that you have some awareness of how you spend your time, the next step is to create a monthly task schedule. (You can buy a large monthly wall calendar at an office supply store and tape it over your desk, or just make one for yourself.) List on the schedule all appointments that are already confirmed, then record all the specific work or school assignments, by client, project, course, etc., that you need to complete in the month. The next step is crucial — post the list where you can see it every day.

Now, move to the next smaller piece of time. Buy a planner that shows the month at a glance — week by week and day by day — to have on your desk, at your workspace, or in your briefcase or knapsack. Transfer information from your monthly wall calendar to the planner (and vice versa), and then add meetings, tasks, etc., as they become known. You're now getting better organized and more aware of what needs to be done — your posted monthly schedule serves as a constant reminder.

As you schedule your days, remember to work some flexibility into your deadlines. It is wise to add a 10 to 20 percent cushion of time to each task so that you are not continually stressed out over upcoming deadlines. Try not to over-schedule yourself; leave yourself plenty of time to avoid arriving late for an appointment.

You should record on these task schedules how closely you held to the time allotted per task and review them periodically. We do, and have found the practice very helpful for future planning and scheduling. You can evaluate how efficiently you are working and how well you are keeping to your schedule. You can discover missed assignments and see what adjustments may need to be made to your planning procedures. Planning properly gives you a sense of your controlling time rather than time controlling you.

ELECTRONIC ORGANIZERS

Of course, in this day and age there are many who are more comfortable dealing with computers and other electronic devices rather than date books, calendars or notepads. For this type of person, organizers such as a Palm Pilot can be extremely efficient. Electronic organizers can store address lists, appointments (some will cover 3 years worth!), "to do" lists, memos, and even expense sheets. The more sophisticated hand-held models can access the Internet and allow you to communicate via e-mail. If electronics are your preference, by all means take advantage of them to keep yourself on schedule and on track. But keep in mind that no device is a substitute for careful, thorough planning.

PRIORITIZE AND CONSOLIDATE

Prioritization can also be a useful tool for staying on top of your schedule and goes a long way toward reducing stress. Learn to differentiate between important, urgent, and "make work" tasks. Tasks which are both important and urgent should be on the top of your task schedule priority list.

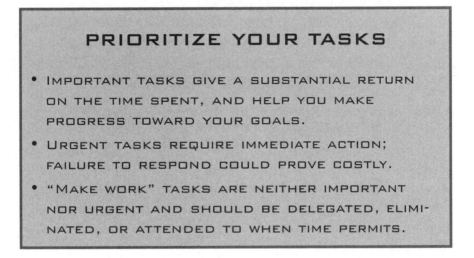

PRIORITIZE YOUR TASKS

- IMPORTANT TASKS GIVE A SUBSTANTIAL RETURN ON THE TIME SPENT, AND HELP YOU MAKE PROGRESS TOWARD YOUR GOALS.
- URGENT TASKS REQUIRE IMMEDIATE ACTION; FAILURE TO RESPOND COULD PROVE COSTLY.
- "MAKE WORK" TASKS ARE NEITHER IMPORTANT NOR URGENT AND SHOULD BE DELEGATED, ELIMINATED, OR ATTENDED TO WHEN TIME PERMITS.

Return to your activity log and note those times during the day when you seem to have the most energy and enthusiasm. Those are the times when important and/or urgent tasks should be undertaken because you will be most focused and efficient. (Some people are morning people; others work best later in the day or evening. Find out when your energy is at its peak.) Once you know the "pulse" of your day, you can try to schedule important meetings or projects, if the option is available, to coincide with your periods of maximum energy.

There are a number of ways to consolidate your efforts and free up more time for those activities which are more important or more interesting. Here are a few time-saving tips that we have adopted:

CONSOLIDATE YOUR EFFORTS (TIME SAVING TIPS)

- ORGANIZE YOUR WORK SPACE AND LIVING SPACE. REDUCE PAPER OVERLOAD: THROW AWAY TRASH MAIL WHEN OPENED; IF YOU MOVE A PIECE OF PAPER AROUND MORE THAN TWICE, FILE OR TOSS IT.

- DO SIMILAR TASKS AT ONE TIME, I.E., TRY TO MAKE PHONE CALLS IN BUNCHES, HANDLE ALL CORRESPONDENCE AT A SITTING, ETC.

- WHEN YOU HAVE AN IMPORTANT OR CREATIVE TASK TO DO, FIND A QUIET WORKPLACE WHERE YOU CAN'T BE DISTURBED. HOLD ALL PHONE CALLS.

- FINISH ONE TASK BEFORE STARTING ANOTHER. IF YOU'RE WORKING ON SEVERAL PROJECTS, DIVIDE THEM INTO SMALLER PORTIONS.

- DO THINGS WHEN THEY COME UP — DON'T PUT THEM OFF.

- TAKE A SPEED-READING COURSE; LEARN TO "READ DOWN."

- LEARN TO SAY "NO" TO ACTIVITIES THAT REDUCE PRODUCTIVITY.

UNDERSTANDING CHANGE

Now that you've scheduled your time better, begun to prioritize your tasks and consolidate your efforts, you must prepare to have your schedule turned upside down by forces beyond your control. Change is the only thing in life that's constant —

all other things are fleeting. All we know in life is that change will happen — whether we are forced to move, get a new job, face unpleasant situations, or deal with health issues. If we become too complacent with the way things are, we are headed for trouble. Understanding change, and devising strategies to adjust your life to it, is a critical element of working with your plan. It's called being flexible — "going with the flow."

Some people accept change and adapt fairly easily; others are temporarily paralyzed by change; still others just refuse to deal with it. Change is important because it can generate positive outcomes. As the old expression says, "When God closes a door, He opens a window."

>☆

Mike: My approach to change in my youth was simple — avoid it at all costs. As a young teacher and coach, I was fortunate to find work at schools that were close enough that I never had to move out of my hometown — Cambridge, Massachusetts. Even when I started my first collegiate head coaching job at Boston University, my commute was short. I only had to cross the bridge over the Charles River to get to my job. Once I obtained the position at B.U., my wife and I started thinking about buying a new home. I gave her only one condition. She could look anywhere for a house — as long as it was in Cambridge!

But you cannot hide from change forever, as I learned some years later when I was offered the head basketball coaching position at George Washington University in Washington, D.C. In considering whether to accept the job, I had to think about leaving behind the security of home, family, and lifelong friends — everything that was familiar.

We also had to leave our son and daughter. We felt that this would be a good time for the kids, both of whom were entering their sophomore year at Boston University, to have a little more space to grow and chart their own life courses. We justified the move to them by saying that it was important not to be afraid to take on new challenges, not to be afraid to make a change, to have courage. We were in the position of having to practice what we preached; what we told the kids was what we were telling ourselves. In the final analysis, my wife and I decided the change would be beneficial both to us and our children, and we committed to the move — even though it was a little scary.

The drive from Cambridge to Washington made us temporarily doubt the wisdom of our choice. With our personal belongings packed in my old "Shoot Straight" van, we headed out. After a stop in Cherry Hill, N.J., the battery died and we had to buy a new one. Then, as we started over the Delaware Memorial Bridge at the end of the New Jersey Turnpike, a thunderstorm of Biblical proportions erupted. It was frightening. Yet we made it through in one piece. My wife summed up our feelings thus: "God didn't send us this far to have us fail now!"

In recalling my fear of making the move to Washington, I wonder now why I was so anxious. The move represented a career advancement, and it turned out to be a positive event for my whole family. I learned that it wasn't about bricks and mortar and familiarity; it was about having faith in yourself, making adjustments and, most of all, about

people. If you can pursue your dreams in the com-
pany of those you love, you will have little fear of the
changes that happen along the way.

WORK WITH A PLAN SUMMARY

There are three important things to remember about planning and time management: 1) they are not a substitute for action; 2) they are an ongoing process; and, 3) they should be flexible.

Legendary UCLA basketball coach John Wooden said, "Failing to prepare is preparing to fail." Remember the key points of working with a game plan for work and for life, and get started, then Wooden's observation will not apply.

WORK WITH A PLAN REMINDERS

- HAVE A PLAN — FOR SCHOOL, WORK, LIFE.
- DO A REALISTIC PERSONAL SKILLS INVENTORY. SET YOUR GOALS DOWN IN WRITING. REVISIT THESE GOALS REGULARLY.
- MAKE YOUR GOALS SPECIFIC, AND ACHIEVABLE WITHIN A TIME FRAME.
- LIST OBJECTIVES TO REACH YOUR GOAL — MAKE THEM PRECISE, FLEXIBLE, AND EASY TO FOLLOW.
- BE PREPARED — HAVE A CONTINGENCY PLAN READY IF THINGS DON'T GO AS EXPECTED.
- UTILIZE TIME MANAGEMENT TECHNIQUES TO SCHEDULE BY MONTH, WEEK, AND DAY — HAVE A DAILY "TO-DO" LIST.
- PRIORITIZE GOALS, OBJECTIVES, AND TASKS; CONSOLIDATE YOUR EFFORTS TO SAVE TIME.
- CHANGE HAPPENS — BE RECEPTIVE TO THE POSITIVE SIDE OF CHANGE.

WORK WITH A PLAN QUESTIONS

1. What goals — short term and long term — can I
   set for myself?

   Short Term   **Long Term**

   _____   _____
   _____   _____
   _____   _____
   _____   _____
   _____   _____

2. What steps can I take to achieve these goals?

   _____
   _____
   _____
   _____
   _____

3. List all those things I want to accomplish in
   the next month.

   _____
   _____
   _____
   _____
   _____

MATTERS OF MONEY

"REMEMBER, THERE ARE ONLY TWO WAYS TO ACHIEVE
FINANCIAL SECURITY — MAKE MORE THAN YOU SPEND
OR SPEND LESS THAN YOU MAKE."

— THE AUTHORS (WE'VE LEARNED THE HARD WAY!)

MANY OF US FAIL WHEN IT COMES TO FINANCIAL LIT-
ERACY. WE DO NOT KNOW NEARLY ENOUGH ABOUT
MANAGING, INVESTING, OR SAVING OUR MONEY.
NOR ARE WE VERY GOOD AT BUDGETING. IT IS
IMPORTANT TO UNDERSTAND FINANCES AND
BECOME ADEPT AT HANDLING MONEY.

WE ARE NOT ECONOMISTS OR MONEY EXPERTS
BUT OVER THE YEARS WE HAVE DISCOVERED SOME
METHODS FOR MAINTAINING OR IMPROVING OUR FIS-
CAL STABILITY. DISCUSSIONS OF MONEY MATTERS
CAN BE RATHER DRY, NEVERTHELESS WE HOPE YOU
WILL GAIN A BETTER UNDERSTANDING OF PERSONAL
FINANCES, AND PERHAPS ACHIEVE SOME FINANCIAL
PEACE OF MIND IN THE PROCESS.

WHERE DOES THE MONEY GO?

This is a question we have all asked ourselves at one time or another. The concept of living within your means seems to have been overruled in recent years by escalating salaries and the proliferation of "pre-approved" credit cards. It is wise, however, to remember that high times are inevitably followed by bad times, when you need something for that "rainy day." Creating a budget and controlling spending are two strategies that will enable you to achieve financial peace of mind. Yes, you may have to put off non-essential purchases until you have the ready cash. But careful management of your finances can reduce money worries that generate incredible stress.

KEEPING TRACK OF YOUR FINANCES

The key to analyzing where your money goes is maintaining accurate records. Set up simple systems that enable you to check if a bill has been paid and plan ahead to see what expenses are coming up. Buy some regular file folders and use them for storing bank statements, utility bills, insurance bills, tax returns, etc. After you balance your checkbook each month, put the statement in the "bank statement" folder. When you pay your bills, note both the date you paid it and the check number used. Then, file them in the appropriate folder. This way, if the electric company wants to turn off your lights, you can easily prove you paid the bill!

Timely payment of bills is a must in order to maintain a clean credit record; mail bills to arrive by the due date that is printed on the invoice. One way to keep on track is to get a calendar that marks the year week by week. As your bills arrive, place them in the book in the week *before* they are due. Write the checks then and mail them for timely payment. When that week comes up, you will have a fairly good idea of what your cash outflow will be and you will always pay on time. Simple, but effective!

⤳☆

Mike: I learned a valuable lesson about paying bills on time — the hard way! When I was growing up in Cambridge, shopping malls and supermarkets were not as numerous as they are today. All of our shopping — groceries, clothes, haircuts, etc. — was done through local merchants. Buying on credit had a much different connotation then.

Credit in those days was between the local merchant and the customer. I could go into a local store, pick up a loaf of bread, and the storekeeper would add it to my mother's account. Each week, she would pay down whatever amount she could. There was no such thing as an invoice, or a 30–60–90 day payment schedule, or an interest charge.

When my wife and I purchased our first home, we borrowed the down payment from family members and mortgaged the balance. Our monthly payment for principal, interest, and real estate taxes was only $232. Of course, my annual salary was only $6,200! We made our payments every month, but because of my ignorance of the concept of credit ratings, we did not always pay the mortgage, or our other bills, on time.

After I accepted the head coaching position at Boston University, we decided to purchase a larger home. This is when the failure to pay bills on time really came back to haunt us. The new bank ran a credit check that indicated we were categorized as a bad credit risk. We could not understand our rating, since all of our bills were paid. But, and this is a big but, they weren't always paid on time; every late payment became a part of our credit history. We finally got the loan, but it was an anxious time.

If you take away only one piece of advice from this chapter, let it be — pay your bills on time!

Once a year has gone by, you can discard invoices such as electric and telephone bills (unless you claim them as a business expense for tax purposes). However, you should have a permanent file box in which to store bank statements (with cancelled checks), insurance policies, loan statements, and old tax returns. You can file other important papers in this box as well: birth certificate, passport, diplomas, etc. It is also important to hang on to receipts from any purchases that have a warranty, so you will have proof if a defect occurs while the warranty is still in effect. It's about getting organized and knowing where things are.

TRACK SPENDING AND CREATE A BUDGET

The time to start paying attention to your money is *now*. Take stock of your spending habits by keeping a diary of expenditures for one month. Track everything you spend your money on in that time — no matter how large or small the amount. Include bus fare, out-of-pocket expenses — no expenditure is too insignificant to be recorded.

From the data you have collected, the next step is to construct a chart that will track your monthly income and outgo.

The chart should include the categories shown below. Add or subtract categories to suit your own situation.

MONTHLY FINANCIAL PROFILE

INCOME:

- Salary after taxes   _____
- Part-time work   _____
- Other income sources   _____
      Total Monthly Income   _____

EXPENSES:

- *Home:*

Mortgage/Rent/Condo fees   _____
Utilities (tel./elec./heat)   _____
Homeowners insurance   _____
Maintenance/repairs   _____
Furnishings/Improvements   _____
Real estate taxes   _____

- *Personal:*

Weekly cash needs   _____
Insurance (life/disability)   _____
Education loans   _____
Clothing purchases   _____
Clothing maintenance (cleaning/tailoring)   _____

Toiletries/cosmetics   _____
Hair Care (stylist, hair care supplies)   _____
Fitness (health club fees, equipment)   _____

• *Food:*

Groceries/Specialty markets   _____

Dining out   _____

• **Transportation:**

Car loan payments   _____

Insurance   _____

Taxes (excise, etc.)   _____

Gasoline   _____

Maintenance/repairs   _____

Parking/tolls/taxis   _____

Public transit (subway, bus, train)   _____

• **Medical:**

Health insurance(general/dental/eye)   _____

Professional fees   _____

   (co-pays, physical therapy, etc.)

Drugs (prescription/over the counter)   _____

Eyeglasses/contact lenses   _____

• **Entertainment/Recreation:**

Theatre/movies/sporting events   _____

Subscriptions/video rentals   _____

Vacations/travel   _____

• **Gifts/Charitable Contributions:**   _____

• **Business (if self-employed):**

Office equipment/supplies   _____

Computer(hardware, software, Internet)   _____

Utilities (phone, fax, cell, elec., heat)   _____

Postage/Fedex/UPS _____

Taxi/tolls/parking _____

Travel and entertainment _____

Secretarial/consulting _____

• *Savings/Investments:*

Retirement/pension _____
(Keogh, IRA, 401K)
Regular savings _____

Total Monthly Expenses _____

For expenses that vary from month to month (such as utilities), take an average figure; for expenses which don't change, but are billed annually (e.g., insurance policies), divide the total by 12 to get a monthly average. If you find you are spending more than you are taking in, this overspending will eventually sabotage your financial health, unless you win the lottery!

ANALYZE YOUR INCOME AND OUTGO

Review your chart to find the sink holes of your monthly finances! For those categories in which you're overspending, take steps to cut back. If your subscription expenses seem excessive, borrow newspapers and magazines from the library. Spending too much on gas? Try car pooling or take public transit if it's available. Be creative *but* conservative.

If you have money available at the end of each month, allocate some to savings. The more money you put into savings, the better prepared you'll be to finance emergencies such as a major auto repair job or a personal computer meltdown. Perhaps you want to purchase a new car or build up a nest egg for a down payment on a home.

These goals will be more easily achieved if you make the choice to save right from the start. In the future, when you want to invest some money or start an education fund, your saving habits will be established. Lack of financial discipline can lead to the accumulation of debt and the inability to save and plan for a secure future. We're talking process here, not specifics. Just get into the habit of budgeting and saving.

CONSTRUCTING A BUDGET

Now is the time to use your Monthly Financial Profile to develop a budget. Why have a budget? Because it will highlight both potential trouble spots and ways to make better use of your income. A budget also enables you to check up on how well you are sticking to your spending resolutions. Review your budget AT THE END OF EVERY MONTH!! Acquire smart saving and spending habits to stay within your budget.

SMART SAVING HABITS

- SAVE YOUR CHANGE. DEPOSIT IN THE BANK — IT CAN ADD UP.
- CLIP COUPONS. THEY CAN BE FOUND IN THE NEWSPAPER, ON YOUR PIZZA BOX, OR ON STORE COUNTERS. USE THEM AND TAKE ADVANTAGE OF THE SAVINGS.
- BUY A TRANSIT PASS. MANY TRANSIT SYSTEMS ISSUE MONTHLY PASSES AT A DISCOUNTED RATE.
- WATCH FOR SALES. BUY YOUR HOLIDAY CARDS AND WRAPPING PAPER FOR NEXT YEAR RIGHT AFTER THIS YEAR'S HOLIDAY SEASON; GET SHEETS AND TOWELS DURING "WHITE SALES," ETC.

Mike: My first salaried coaching job paid $600 a year. By 1968, I was earning $6,200 annually as a teacher. We ate a lot of chicken and pasta in those days! When I started earning higher salaries, I found that my "pocket money" didn't increase substantially, because I had to save more, buy insurance, and try to arrange for some financial security in the future. So the low budget meals continued for a while.

Now that we're on a firmer footing financially, we still abide by the lessons we learned in the early days. We keep to a budget, we pay our bills on time, and we know the difference between what we want *and what we* need. *Most importantly, we learned that saving is a financial fundamental. Our financial motto is, "Pay now, play later."*

BANKING BASICS

When you were growing up, you may have had a savings account and when you needed money for something, you just withdrew the amount needed. When you enter the working world full time, you need a better method to manage your cash flow. You need to have a checking account to deposit your paychecks, pay bills, etc. Most banks offer checking accounts and automated teller machines (ATMs). The trick is to find a solid, reputable bank that charges competitive fees for these services. You need not limit your search to neighborhood banks now that electronic banking is available and ATM networks service any number of banks.

During your search for the best bank for you, remember these terms:

BASIC BANKING TERMS

Service fees	Check processing charges and ATM service charges.
ATM fees	The amount charged to your account for transactions at your bank or fees related to another bank's ATM.
Minimum balance	Refers to the amount of money that must be maintained in a checking account in order to avoid any service fees.
NOW account	A checking account that pays minimal interest.

When shopping for a bank, find out what the service and ATM fees are. As far as NOW accounts go, often there are substantial minimum balance requirements that may offset the small amount of interest to be earned. You may be better off paying the fee for checking and earning more interest in a savings account.

When choosing a bank, you must decide whether human contact is unimportant (e.g., at a large "mega-bank") or you prefer the "personal touch" (e.g., a small, neighborhood bank). Ask friends or co-workers if you need guidance. There are also Internet banks available that may offer an attractive alternative.

MANAGE YOUR ACCOUNT

You can use your checking account as a money management tool. If you tend to spend your paycheck as soon as it hits your pocket, have it electronically deposited to your account, if possible. Then, on payday, funds from your paycheck will be automatically sent to your checking account. Not only does this cut down on trips to the bank, it removes the temptation to take "just a little" out of your check for something that might not be a necessity. Some banks will even put a portion of your check directly into a savings account if you ask for the service. Money that you never see is much easier to save!

If electronic deposit is not available to you, stop and think before you cash each paycheck. Use your monthly analysis to determine how much is needed to cover your expenses, and deduct only the amount you will need to get through the week and deposit the remainder. Some jobs will pay you every two weeks, or even monthly, making financial discipline even more important.

BALANCING YOUR ACCOUNT

The importance of balancing your checkbook each month cannot be overstated. Not only will it give you a more accurate picture of your position, it will help guard against "bouncing" checks — writing checks for amounts that are greater than your current balance. Balancing your checking account is not difficult — it just requires addition and subtraction and some discipline.

One way to ease the task is to have the type of checkbook you can carry with you so that you can record every check as you write it. Forgotten checks can come back to haunt you, as can unrecorded ATM transactions. Another piece of advice — get overdraft protection from your bank. It will automatically cover a check for which there are insufficient funds in your account.

ATM Awareness

Careful use of ATM machines is an important factor in managing your money. Many banks charge a fee for their use, even when they are in the bank's network. (Some banks will allow you to avoid these fees by keeping a minimum balance in your checking account.) Virtually all banks charge a fee for use of an ATM that is not in their network. You may also be charged for other ATM services such as checking your balance or transferring money from a checking to a savings account. Advice on use of ATMs can be reduced to these two tips:

- *Limit your use of ATMs — use your cash wisely.*

- *Be sure you know all the fees associated with ATM use.*

"TAKE CREDIT" FOR YOUR DEBT

You may think that the above title is our way of encouraging you to use credit cards. Quite the opposite is true. What we are saying is that you have to be responsible in both the creation and repayment of debt. Obviously, there are some forms of debt that are hard to avoid such as auto loans, mortgages, education loans. But credit card debt can be like quicksand if you are not extremely careful.

Credit Card Caution

It is amazing how many credit card offers come through the mail each month. While it may be tempting to avail yourself of the buying power they allegedly provide, you must always be aware of the long-term consequences — higher interest rates, negative impact on credit rating — that misuse of these financial tools can produce. It is hard to get by without a credit card and they do come in handy in certain situations:

- Purchases can be made without carrying large sums of cash.

- Emergencies such as auto repairs can be handled when sufficient cash is unavailable.

- Some transactions, like guaranteeing a hotel room, require a credit card.

- Credit cards can act as personal identification when trying to cash a check.

- Credit card receipts can help with a dispute over a merchandise return.

Mike: Over the years, I have observed the habits of college students who are using (and abusing) credit cards for the first time. The temptation to overspend is great. Many are unaware that any late payments, or non-payments, will show up on their credit rating. As a young adult I, too, was unaware of the importance of timely payments.

Students' failure to use credit cards wisely can result in their not being allowed to have one at all. Even the simplest financial transactions can be difficult without a credit card (buying on-line or trying to reserve airline or concert tickets). The irony is that when your credit is restored, everyone wants to give you a credit card again! So, take a cautious approach to credit cards and remember this: "Too much of anything is good for nothing."

You can control the effect of credit cards on your financial health by following these rules:

CREDIT CARD CAUTION

- LIMIT THE NUMBER OF CREDIT CARDS YOU HAVE. NO MORE THAN TWO IS YOUR BEST BET.

- UNDERSTAND THE TERMS AND CONDITIONS. GET THE LOWEST INTEREST RATE, AND LEARN THE CONSEQUENCES OF NOT PAYING THE FULL BALANCE EACH MONTH.

- TRY TO PAY YOUR FULL BALANCE EACH MONTH. IF YOU CANNOT, PAY AS MUCH AS YOU CAN BY THE DUE DATE TO MINIMIZE INTEREST CHARGES AND MAINTAIN A GOOD CREDIT RATING.

- DO NOT CHARGE WHAT YOU CANNOT AFFORD. IF A PURCHASE COULD BE DEFERRED, OR IS NON-ESSENTIAL — STOP AND THINK. DON'T "BUST THE BUDGET" UNLESS IT'S ABSOLUTELY NECESSARY.

UNDERSTANDING LOANS

The way to pay less on auto loans and mortgages is to search for the lowest interest rates. Investigate a number of banks, credit unions, or other credit sources before applying for a loan. For mortgages, also consider banks that do not charge "points" or have lower or no closing costs.

As with credit card debt, timely payments are a must on any loans. If at any time you have some funds available and wish to pay off a loan, by all means do so if there are no pre-payment penalties. It is always a good idea to pay a little extra in those months you can, so that the overall loan term can be shortened. Also, note that mortgage interest payments and some education loan interest payments are tax deductible.

INSURE YOUR FUTURE

It is wise to pay attention to health, auto, disability, house/ apartment, and even life insurance. Premiums may cut into your monthly spending allowance, but they are necessary to guard against a problem that could shake your financial foundation. Ask a trusted advisor where to start.

HEALTH INSURANCE

Many employers provide health insurance for which premium costs become a payroll deduction — no muss, no fuss. For those who are self-employed or work for small businesses that cannot provide insurance coverage, the challenge is greater. Many insurance carriers will not allow an individual to enroll unless he or she is a member of a larger group. The key is to find a group (an affinity group) of which you can become a member and then obtain coverage. Examples of such groups are: Chambers of Commerce, professional organizations, auto clubs, alumni associations, military organizations, etc. Your state insurance department and the Internet can be good sources of information.

When you find an insurance policy for which you are eligible, learn everything you can about the coverage they offer. Get information on:

- *Waiting periods*

- *Coverage of pre-existing conditions*

- *Amount of deductible*

- *Prescription drug coverage*

- *How emergencies are handled*

- *Excluded medical conditions*

- *Maternity and pediatric coverage*

Health insurance is something you cannot do without; get the most comprehensive coverage you can afford.

Auto Insurance

There are four types of automobile insurance coverage:

Liability	*if you injure someone or damage something*
Medical	*if you or someone else is injured in an auto accident*
Collision	*damage to your car from hitting something*
Comprehensive	*damage from theft, fire or natural causes, i.e., flood, hurricane, etc.*

Different states have various mandatory coverage requirements; check what your state demands. Then find an insurance company that offers the best coverage at the lowest cost. Inquire if discounts apply for such things as: a good driving record; a good academic record; safety features of the car; or, being a member of an affinity group (as mentioned in the health insurance section).

DISABILITY INSURANCE

Disability insurance is an expense item that few people take into consideration. But, think about it — if you are disabled and cannot work for a lengthy period of time, how will you survive financially, particularly if you are self-employed? For those of you who are on your own, disability insurance should be a part of your insurance package. (Keep in mind that Workman's Compensation [government coverage] only applies to incidents which happen while *on the job.*)

If disability is not included in your employment benefits, shop around for the policy that offers the highest percentage of salary, covers both accidental and illness-related disability, does not require annual physicals for renewal, is non-cancellable, and will reimburse for a partial as well as total disability.

LIFE INSURANCE

The first thing to understand about life insurance is that "term" life insurance will pay the face value of the policy to your beneficiary on your death. "Whole" life insurance invests a portion of your premium payments, building up a cash value. The premiums for whole life insurance are typically higher than for term life.

Many would say that unless you are married and/or have some dependents, life insurance is not necessary. That may be true, but it is also important to remember that the younger you are when you take out a life insurance policy, the less expensive the premiums will be over the life of the policy. Also, whole life could represent a form of savings plan for those who are less disciplined about saving. It is something to think about if you feel you will not be able to set aside a regular amount to invest in a retirement plan of some sort.

★

Mike: Often young people simply neglect to think about life insurance or put off purchase of a policy until later in life. The story of Malik Sealy will demonstrate the danger of such inaction.

Malik Sealy was a star basketball player and graduate of St. John's University. He went on to the NBA, played for a number of teams, and began the 1999–2000 season with the Minnesota Timberwolves. He was on the verge of realizing his full professional potential, both in performance and compensation.

Malik was not just a basketball player, however. He took an active role in his community and had a number of business interests. When Malik spoke at basketball camps, he would tell his young audiences that the three things in life you had to be were: a good person, a good student, and a good athlete, in that order. Malik had recently started a clothing line and was hoping to open his own recording studio. This was a young person who was balancing his physical, mental, and spiritual sides.

The news of Malik's death in May 2000 at the hands of a drunk driver was devastating. Malik was just thirty years old. He was survived by a wife and a three-year-old son. What he failed to leave behind was any life insurance. Obviously, he would not deliberately have jeopardized his family's financial health, but his failure to have any insurance on his life made their situation less secure. His story is an important object lesson for young people who think life insurance is for "old folks."

★

MATTERS OF MONEY SUMMARY

It would be nice if we were all the beneficiaries of a trust fund worth millions of dollars. As that is not generally the case, we have to be careful how we manage our finances. If you keep in mind our advice about making more than you spend, or spending less than you make, your matters of money will be far less complicated.

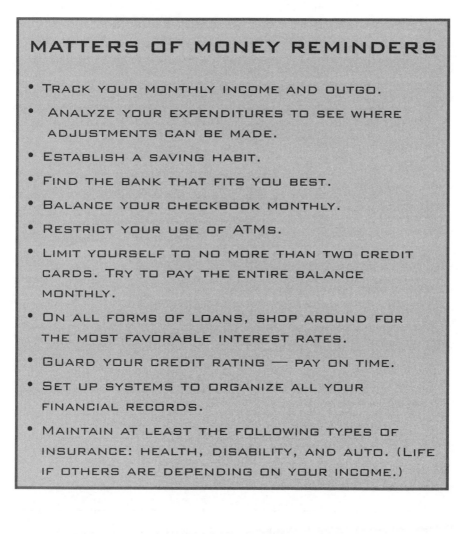

MATTERS OF MONEY REMINDERS

- Track your monthly income and outgo.
- Analyze your expenditures to see where adjustments can be made.
- Establish a saving habit.
- Find the bank that fits you best.
- Balance your checkbook monthly.
- Restrict your use of ATMs.
- Limit yourself to no more than two credit cards. Try to pay the entire balance monthly.
- On all forms of loans, shop around for the most favorable interest rates.
- Guard your credit rating — pay on time.
- Set up systems to organize all your financial records.
- Maintain at least the following types of insurance: health, disability, and auto. (Life if others are depending on your income.)

MATTERS OF MONEY QUESTIONS

1. Do I have a monthly budget? If not, what steps
   can I take to prepare and use a budget?

   _____

   _____

   _____

   _____

   _____

2. What are my financial goals and how will I get there?

   _____

   _____

   _____

   _____

   _____

3. What do I need to do to organize my financial records
   more efficiently?

   _____

   _____

   _____

   _____

   _____

WHERE DO YOU GO FROM HERE?

GIVING BACK

If you want happiness for an hour
. . . take a nap.
If you want happiness for a day
. . . go fishing.
If you want happiness for a year
. . . inherit a fortune.
If you want happiness for a lifetime
. . . help somebody.

— Chinese Proverb

When we close our Skills for Life presentations, we caution our audiences that there are two absolute necessities in life — to pay your taxes and to give back. Former First Lady Barbara Bush once said, "Some people give time, some money, some their skills and connections, some literally give their life's blood. But everyone has something to give." This is where you come in.

If you were not taught as a child the importance of helping others, then giving back is an exercise that may take a little getting used to. First, you have to get over the feeling that you have nothing worthwhile to contribute. Then you have to decide who might benefit the most from what you can give. Are you an avid cyclist? Ride in a road race for a charitable cause. Can you play a sport particularly well? Volunteer at a YMCA/YWCA or Boys and Girls Club or coach a youth team. Do you get along with young people and identify with the problems of growing up? Become a Big Sister or Big Brother. Do you like to read aloud? Tape books for the blind.

⭐

Mike: My mother was the first person to instill in me the need to give back. Given our strained financial status, one would think that there would be little for us to contribute. But Mom was always the first to say that there must be something we had that could be used by someone else needier than we were. Even pants that had been patched up four or five times could be given to someone less fortunate.

From her example, I started to understand at an early age the concept of giving back, of sharing whatever you had to offer to someone in the community who might need it. It could be your voice in a church choir, an offering of food to a family grieving the death of a loved one, or a note of thanks to a teacher or another who has done you a good turn. It didn't matter whether you were young or old, rich or poor — it was your duty and privilege to share your special gift with others.

⭐

MAKING IT WORK

Giving back doesn't necessarily have to be associated with a large organization, nor do you need to be center stage if it makes you feel uncomfortable. Can you stack canned goods? See if your local food pantry needs staffing. Can you stuff envelopes? Get involved in a group that serves some worthwhile interest in your community. Can you rake or shovel? Help your elderly neighbors with removal of leaves or snow. There are so many ways to lend a helping hand. On the next page, we suggest some volunteer efforts to help start you thinking about how you can contribute. You might also call your local United Way or browse Web sites such as www.volunteersolution.org, which lists volunteer openings for select American urban areas. The needs are great and the opportunities are limitless — and when you give of yourself, you'll feel good.

Social position, financial status, or educational level do not determine the value of the contribution you might make. Good causes would fall by the wayside if they had to depend only on the rich or powerful to lend a hand. It is the sharing of time and talent at the most basic levels — neighborhood, community, or house of worship — by people from all walks of life that makes our world and our country better and more civilized places to live. The more successful you are, however, the greater the obligation to share your knowledge, time or money with those who have not had similar opportunities. "Service is the rent we pay for living" according to Marian Wright Edelman, founder of the Children's Defense Fund.

GET STARTED ON GIVING BACK
PARTIAL LIST OF VOLUNTEER OPPORTUNITIES

DISEASE/DISABILITY

- Record books for the blind
- Work for Special Olympics
- Support a cancer patient
- Work at a camp for disabled children

SENIORS

- Volunteer at nursing homes
- Drive patients to doctor appointments
- Deliver "Meals on Wheels"
- Work at a Senior Center

YOUTH

- Join Big Brother/Big Sister
- Volunteer at the Boys & Girls Clubs
- Be a YMCA or YWCA after-school tutor
- Mentor at-risk teens

FAMILIES IN CRISIS

- Tutor homeless children
- Staff a battered spouse shelter
- Work at a local food pantry
- Volunteer at a parental stress hotline

CHILDREN

- Work in public schools
- Promote early childhood literacy
- Make blankets for the needy
- Read to children in the hospital

Sports

- Coach a local youth team
- Referee youth league games
- Work on a youth league committee
- Help with fundraising

Adult Education/Literacy

- Join your library's literacy program
- Teach English as a Second Language
- Tutor GED students
- Volunteer at a welfare-to-work program

Other

- Be a hospice volunteer
- Be a tour guide at an historical site
- Help out at an animal shelter
- Work for Habitat for Humanity

The Benefits

The return on investment which accrues to society from the practice of giving back is substantial. The corporation that supports a mentoring program for young people creates a group of skilled workers. The young person who volunteers in a literacy program improves the self-respect of those who are tutored. A university student-athlete who encourages youngsters from the community to think about college gives them a broader outlook on their future. Someone who gathers sponsors for a walk against hunger makes strides toward eradicating one of the most difficult problems facing the world today. Everyone benefits in some way, shape, or form from the unselfish efforts of those who recognize the need to give back.

The greatest benefit of giving back falls on the person engaged in the activity. The personal satisfaction that comes from knowing you have made a difference is tremendous. Giving back has other benefits as well. For example, if you are thinking of the welfare of others, you will not focus so closely on yourself and your "issues." Problems you may be grappling with lose their power to overwhelm when you think about the problems faced by those whom you are trying to help. As the old saying goes, "I felt bad that I had no shoes until I met a man who had no feet."

꩜

Mike: A very close friend of mine — a person I respect greatly — ran into a difficult time recently. He ran the gamut of personal problems — job loss, financial insecurity, divorce, illness. His reactions ranged from denial to depression to procrastination.

During this difficult period, a group of his friends got together with him for an intense advice session. The assistance and ultimate networking paid off, resulting in a new position for my friend. He's now back to his old self, only better.

While he was in the midst of his troubles, he came to the realization that not only did he need more faith, but he needed to get out of himself and concentrate on others. He volunteered at the local YMCA, gave advice to young people on joining the working world, and devoted at least one day per week to someone other than himself.

Today I have more respect than ever for this man because, during one of the toughest periods of his life,

he realized that giving back can be just as therapeutic
for the donor as for the recipient.

Beyond the improved perspective to be had from giving back, there is a more practical reason to do so. Volunteer work can be a showcase for your particular skills. Many people supporting worthy causes have "day jobs"; some may even be business owners or influential executives. Impress them with your work ethic, loyalty, and responsibility, and they just might think of you first when a position opens up at their place of work. The volunteers with whom you work will also become members of your network.

Not only can volunteer work showcase your skills, but it can provide an opportunity to learn new ones. For example, if the cause needs someone to maintain its computerized list of contributors, take on the job. You can learn about database management that way. Or, if the organization wants to send stories to local newspapers about an event, offer to write the press release. You can use the opportunity to perfect your writing skills. Getting involved in the planning of a charitable event will teach you attention to detail, follow-through, and the importance of meeting deadlines. By helping others, you can help yourself become more competent and confident – not a bad deal.

GIVING BACK QUESTIONS

1. What is the best way for me to give back and how can I begin?

   _____

   _____

   _____

   _____

2. How will giving back help me?

   _____

   _____

   _____

   _____

3. Who are my heroes? Which of their character traits do I most admire?

   _____

   _____

   _____

   _____

THE BEST YOU CAN BE

"LIFE IS A DECATHLON — YOU MUST BE GOOD
AT MORE THAN ONE EVENT."

— MICHAEL J. McGOVERN, ESQ.

NOW WE RETURN TO MICHAEL McGOVERN'S QUOTE THAT STARTED THE BOOK — "LIFE IS A DECATHLON" — TO DESCRIBE THE FINAL EVENT OF **SKILLS FOR LIFE.** SUCCESS IN THIS EVENT — BECOMING **THE BEST YOU CAN BE** — REQUIRES THAT YOU DRAW UPON ALL OF THE OTHER SKILLS DESCRIBED IN THE BOOK. MASTERING THE FUNDAMENTALS YOU NEED TO SUCCEED CAN MAKE YOUR PERSONAL DECATHLON A RICH AND FULFILLING EXPERIENCE.

Is it time to put this book on the shelf and let it gather dust? No. We think *Skills for Life* should be an ongoing exercise, because becoming the best person you can be is a lifelong effort. The information we provide will be useless unless it is put into practice on a regular basis. Practice, practice, practice may seem like a boring refrain, but little success can be achieved without it.

Mike: In the "Getting Along" chapter, I mention that one of my childhood mentors was Stretch Headley, coach of the Cardullo's Little League team of which I was a member. Stretch was a firm believer in the "practice makes permanent" philosophy. At every practice, he would hit hundreds of infield grounders and pop flies to sharpen our fielding skills.

Everything Stretch did was purposeful, and he was at his best at those practices following a loss. He would return to the fundamentals and tell us that the value of the loss was how it exposed those areas in which we needed to improve. He knew that we would lose again, but he felt that the gap between losses would grow larger as we worked on making our skills a permanent part of our game. For him, practice was the only way to become the best ballplayer you could be.

We believe that the same philosophy holds true with the skills for life presented in this book. Practicing and making them a permanent part of your being will help you become the best person you can be.

We want this book to become a reference for the reader to return to frequently. Once you have completed your first reading of the chapter(s) covering the areas you felt needed improvement, begin to incorporate the tips into your daily life. After some time has passed, ask yourself, your mentor, or someone whom you respect, whether any positive changes in the way you conduct yourself are evident. Below are some questions to help you assess your progress:

WHO YOU ARE

Character:
Am I still searching for the easy way out?
Do I have a tendency to stretch the truth?

Attitude:
Do I let negative feelings get me down?
Do I see the glass as half empty rather than half full?

Getting Along:
Do I treat everyone with respect?
Do I know what it means to be a friend?

Spirituality:
Am I too much concerned with material things?
Do I do things that add spiritual meaning to my life?

HOW YOU LOOK

Appearance and Costume:	*Do I always look clean and neat?* *Am I in good shape?* *Do I dress for the occasion?* *Do I wear styles appropriate to my age and body type?*

HOW YOU PERFORM

Basic Communication:	*Can I present my ideas clearly?* *Do I listen well? Attentively?*
Work with a Plan:	*Do I have a plan for today, tomorrow and the future?* *Do I make daily lists?* *Am I able to adapt to change?*
Matters of Money:	*Do I know where my money goes?* *Do I stay within my budget?* *Am I saving money?*

WHERE DO YOU GO FROM HERE?

Giving Back:	*Do I try to share my special gifts with others?* *Do I think about other's welfare or am I totally self-absorbed?*

If you're unhappy with the answers to these questions, go back to the chapter, review the skills, and then practice, practice, practice the skills until the fundamentals become almost automatic. Even the people who seem the most successful could not have achieved their goals without frequently evaluating their mastery of these Skills for Life.

You can use the Personal Inventory from the beginning of the book to assess how well you are perfecting each skill for life. Tabulate your score in each section of the inventory as follows:

Score By Section:

16: You're a master of this *skill for life*.
13–15: Just a little tune-up required.
9–12: More improvement needed.
5–8: Concentrate on areas that need work.
0–4: Ask for help.

Remember to be honest with yourself when answering the questions so that your scores reflect an accurate profile of your current status. Otherwise, the exercise will not produce the intended results.

Mike: A friend of mine sent me a copy of a poem, which sums up the Skills for Life commitment to being the best you can be quite nicely. If we all were to keep the promises to ourselves expressed in "Promise Yourself," we would probably be better, happier people, and our personal inventory scores would always fall in the "master of this skill for life" range.

PROMISE YOURSELF

To be so strong that nothing can disturb your peace of mind.

To talk health, happiness and prosperity to every person you meet.

To make all your friends feel that there is something in them.

To look at the sunny side of everything and make your optimism come true.

To think only of the best, to work only for the best, and expect only the best.

To be just as enthusiastic about the success of others as you are about your own.

To forget the mistakes of the past and press on to the greater achievements of the future.

To wear a cheerful countenance at all times and give every living creature you meet a smile.

To give so much time to the improvement of yourself that you have no time to criticize others.

To be too large for worry, too noble for anger, too strong for fear, and too happy to permit the presence of trouble.

To think well of yourself and to proclaim this fact to the world, not in loud words, but in great deeds.

To live in the faith that the whole world is on your side as long as you are true to the best that is in you.

C. D. Larson
Your Forces and How to Use Them

We have taken great pleasure in spreading our skills for life philosophy far and wide. We have met some impressive people, people who want to make the most of their lives, to make an impact, and to feel personal satisfaction. We are sure that the readers of this book will be similar in their desire to improve themselves, experience success, and carve out a life with meaning. All of the material presented in *Skills for Life* is directed toward achieving those goals. We hope that it will inspire and then motivate its readers to make each day as productive as possible.

Skills for Life can only serve as a road map, however. You have to embark on the journey by yourself, and approach each landmark along the way on your own. For years, we have told our audiences that regardless of how many books you read, or how many mentors may advise you, or how much education you might acquire, life boils down to one thing — taking responsibility for yourself. To drive this point home, we conclude each Skills for Life session we present with a work by nineteenth-century English poet, William Ernest Henley, titled *Invictus*. Henley's poetry reflects his courage as a man who persevered and succeeded despite a bout with tuberculosis of the bone, which necessitated the amputation of a foot, and the death of his only child, a daughter, at the age of six.

The last two lines of *Invictus*: "I am the master of my fate, I am the captain of my soul," reinforce Henley's and our belief that becoming the best you can be is an individual pursuit that may involve overcoming difficult circumstances. Making the most of your work, your relationships, your life, your very being is, in large part, in your hands alone. Life is not always easy; the choice of how to meet and overcome its challenges is up to you.

Writing a book is never easy, but meaningful pursuits rarely are. We stayed the course because we felt that we had something of value to share. If any readers reap some benefit from our effort, we will be extremely gratified. Their victories, whether large or small, will be our reward.

In closing, we would like to leave you with a brief summary of the guiding principles of the Skills for Life philosophy. Keep them in mind as you embark on your individual journeys. We wish you the best that life has to offer — satisfying work, supportive relationships, the joy that comes from helping others. Create the richest life experience you can for yourself.

10 FUNDAMENTALS FOR SUCCESS

CHARACTER
Character defines who you are — be the one who always tries to do the right thing.

ATTITUDE
Be inspired — think, act, work, play, dream, laugh, and love with enthusiasm.

GETTING ALONG
Make someone feel important every day, including yourself.

SPIRITUALITY
God has given every one of us a special gift — discover it, use it, and share it.

APPEARANCE/COSTUME
Appearance doesn't make the person, but it does make a difference. In the game of life, you have to know what uniform to wear.

BASIC COMMUNICATION
Speak well . . . but listen better.

WORK WITH A PLAN
You cannot reach your destination unless you know where you are going. Plan your work and life and then work your plan.

MATTERS OF MONEY
Spend wisely, save well, and pay your bills on time.

GIVING BACK
Make this world a better place — be of service.

THE BEST YOU CAN BE
Work on your fundamentals every day.

EPILOGUE

It is one thing to convey to others a formula for improving one's situation in life (*Skills for Life: The Fundamentals You Need to Succeed*). It is quite another to adhere to these principles yourself on a daily basis. The truth is we're all human, and sometimes we falter, particularly when faced with difficult situations.

As we moved toward completion of the book, we reflected on the year's challenges and were made more mindful than ever of the importance of the fundamentals we were presenting. One example was the St. John's 2002–2003 basketball campaign. It had a hopeful beginning, experienced a stormy middle, but came to a victorious conclusion. The season provided proof that *Skills for Life* works, if you simply concentrate on the fundamentals and stay with the program.

⭐

Mike: *The season began with great expectations, (much like our 2000–2001 "learning, not losing season") with a 5–0 record giving rise to hopeful thoughts of a championship. The death of my brother, Richard, in early December seemed to launch a downward spiral and, with expectation not being mirrored in reality, we struggled to a 12–12 record.*

Some element of a winning formula was missing. A number of possibilities — we overrated our talent, team chemistry was off, coaches were not communicating effectively enough with the players — might have been at play. Clearly, something wasn't as it should be. Some of our spectators became critical, calling for my resignation and even booing the players when they fell behind or failed to play up to expectations.

At no time did the coaches or players succumb to the pressure — we still believed in ourselves. We continued to work on the fundamentals, refining our approach, and restoring the self-confidence necessary for an end-of-season run. On a bus trip during this period, the team watched the movie "Hardball," the story of an inner-city little league team that prevails in the face of incredible adversity. A key line of the movie's script — "The most important thing in life is showing up." — summarized our approach and dedication to the rest of the season.

We took our .500 record to Madison Square Garden and a CBS "Sunday Game of the Week" against tenth-ranked Duke, which was nationally telecast. CBS was concerned with the match-up, and feared the Red Storm would be soundly beaten (always bad for ratings). In one of the most memorable games ever played at Madison Square Garden, St. John's defeated Duke, via a Marcus Hatten no-time-left free throw, and thus began a stretch run of nine victories in ten games.

Few of the coaches, players, or fans had ever been

*on such an unbelievable ride. The team earned a bid
to the National Invitational Tournament (NIT), and
claimed the NIT title at Madison Square Garden by
defeating Bobby Knight's Texas Tech team in the
semi-finals and Georgetown in the finals. A week
after winning a record sixth NIT championship for
St. John's, the team was invited to ring the opening
bell at the New York Stock Exchange before a TV
audience of some 150 million people. The Red Storm
went from bums to the toast of the town in a matter
of a month. Needless to say, the memories from this
season will last a lifetime.*

The 2002–2003 St. John's basketball team — players and
coaches — put almost all of our skills for life to use. They:
overcame adversity (*Character*); stayed positive and determined (*Attitude*); attempted to interact with one another more
effectively (*Getting Along*); placed their trust and faith in a
power greater than themselves (*Spirituality*); enhanced their
level of fitness (*Appearance and Costume*); communicated
better during practices and games, as well as in the locker
room (*Basic Communication*); improved their execution
(*Work With A Plan*); and, gave 100 percent all the time (*The
Best You Can Be*). They showed up every day and played each
minute as if it were their last. We can think of no stronger tes-
tament to the power of skills for life, and the fundamentals
you need to succeed.

ABOUT THE AUTHORS

MIKE JARVIS has been teaching and coaching basketball since graduating from Northeastern University in 1967. During his tenure as head coach at Cambridge Rindge & Latin High School (Cambridge, MA), he led his teams to three consecutive State Championships and a number one national ranking. He is one of only four college coaches, and the only active coach who has won 100 games or more at three or more different schools. (The other three are Lefty Driesel, Tom Davis, and Jerry Tarkanian.) His college teams — Boston University, George Washington University, and St. John's University — have had numerous NCAA Men's Basketball Tournament appearances as well. As a teacher-coach, Mike's philosophy has always been to prepare his young players for the larger game — the game of life.

JONATHAN PECK is a management consultant with over thirty-five years of experience serving small- and medium-size organizations, *Fortune* 500 companies, and government agencies. He has founded and run several successful businesses. He specializes in communications consulting, new business development, and strategic/business planning. He is a speechwriter and presentation trainer/coach and has taught at the Boston University Graduate School of Management.

The authors have been colleagues and friends for over eighteen years in a relationship marked by mutual respect and their conviction that all of us can use a helping hand from time to time. Their complementary mentoring, teaching, and coaching capabilities lend a unique depth and breadth to the lessons presented in *Skills for Life*.